SILENCE,
EXILE
AND
CUNNING

SILENCE, EXILE AND CUNNING

Memoir of a Life at Work

Jack Oakley

URTEXT
San Rafael

Book and cover design by Glenn Claycomb.
Cover photography by Maryam Pirnazar.

ISBN: 978-1-940121-00-0

Published by Urtext
San Rafael, California
www.urtext.us

Printed in the United States of America

Prologue

PART I
Finding a Job

PART II
Learning the Job

PART III
Trying To Do the Job

I will tell you what I will do and what I will not do. I will not serve that in which I no longer believe, whether it call itself my home, my fatherland, or my church: and I will try to express myself in some mode of life or art as wholly as I can and as freely as I can, using for my defence the only arms I allow myself to use—silence, exile and cunning.

Stephen Dedalus

Bummer

This book is a downer. I always wanted to write a novel you could enter from the cold outside, open the door to the vestibule, stamp the snow off your boots and walk into a warm friendly kitchen to join us around the cast-iron stove, contentedly roll a cigarette and talk about the plumbing to be done or the pictures to be developed or the sorrow of mortality and the ineffability of beauty—but this is what I'm stuck with: a book about work, white-collar middle class white boss work in America.

Jobs Erode

Monday through Friday eight to five or more if they want it, week after week after week. You've just discovered archery or gardening or your kid's class is going camping—forget it, you haven't got the time. Mornings when you're fresh and afternoons when you're reflective are spent at the office. Your best energies are not spent on what you want to do as the hours and months and years go by.

The same thing over and over. Some tasks are assigned simply to keep you busy, you think; and no matter how well and how fast you do what's needed, god forbid that you don't look busy. Even the best jobs, more or less independent work on complicated one-of-a-kind projects, have their longueurs and repetitions, though you sometimes take some solace in the thought that in the end you'll take some satisfaction in having accomplished something.

Fear as a Management Tool

You're always afraid of losing your job. If you ask for too much or don't seem to be working hard enough, you're made aware that others would be happy to have it. The media prod your anxiety with articles about the never-ending economic crisis, the Social Security disaster, the pension bust, the human interest stories about this family learning to love self-employment after layoff and that one furnishing a small apartment on a low budget.

Keep 'em scared! The terrorists are at your door! No liquids on the airplanes and no jokes in security! Don't talk to strangers! Don't look them in the eye! You're a bum if your kid doesn't go to college! Your kid won't go to college unless he gets into the right preschool! A vote for my opponent is a vote for anarchy! Shut up and work!

Work is a Ripoff

You're paid as little as they can get away with. There aren't many good engineers around and employers recognize that they can move to a competing firm for a meager bit more if not forestalled by a meager annual raise. To get a larger one you can mention how much someplace else is paying new hires, but they resent these hints and it works only once or twice. Your only significant raises come when you do move.

But each time you move, you start over with two weeks' vacation that you can't begin to take until six months pass. (You can't try to save your crummy two weeks for a few years to get a decent vacation because you can't accumulate more than four weeks.) You lose the miniscule sick leave that you didn't use. You lose any ESOP shares you had, and you lose the unvested portion of the company's contribution to your 401(k).

That's another ripoff—401(k)s instead of pensions.

Retirement is up to you. The notion is outdated that a company will succor you a bit for your loyalty when you can't give them the work you always did. You're on your own with your 401(k) and its value fluctuates to benefit the traders.

You work overtime for free. Blue-collar jobs have their own ways of extorting unpaid labor. In the professions it works like this: First, you're an exempt employee, exempt from being paid overtime, that is. You see, you're paid a salary and your job is more secure than a laborer's. That's a good one. I'd like to know who ran that through the legislatures. Next, you do what it takes to do the job. Skip lunch, work nights and weekends to meet a deadline. Your training begins with college all-nighters. Then you're hired and young and excited and want to prove your dedication, show off your talents. This is fine for the owner with a fixed fee project, but not so fine for the employees on a fixed monthly wage. And with the trend toward internship you work for free just to get your first paying job. Remember those darling medieval apprenticeships? They're coming back. Soon you'll be paying for your internship.

The unions have capitulated—if they ever did care more about workers than cozying up to owners. Bargaining is a matter of negotiating smaller cuts. Mr. Union Man Samuel Gompers: "The worst crime against working people is a company which fails to operate at a profit." Does it follow that the best crime against working people is operating at the biggest profit? The owners liked Mr. Gompers. They still do. The town next to good old radical Berkeley named a new high school after him!

Why Work?

Ever watch a lion? It gets up when it's time to eat, or mate, or defend its young. Otherwise it lies around conserving energy. It will also play, especially when young. Animals need to learn and exercise their physical and social skills so their readiness is at its peak when survival is at stake. But your typical animal only works when it must, and work ends when it drags down some food—but if I quit my job, I won't find another walking by the next time I'm hungry. I must not cease from working.

Propaganda

A basic element of social propaganda in America—where each individual must build his own career from scratch and work without cease to cobble together a few small holdings to share with his children for a start of their own, not that this differs much from the birds who build their nests each spring to attract a mate whilst avoiding hawks and badgers (each creature faces its own exigencies, though we humans have somewhat transcended the struggle for mere existence)—is that it's your own fault if you don't prosper, you're uneducated, you can't find a job, your job went to Mexico, and you're poor. As in all half-convincing lies, there is some truth in some of this—possibilities do exist for the ambitious, the resolute and the stout.

What then are the flaws in promising young people who though possessed of health, talent and financial support don't achieve the career success for which they seem bound? This one smokes pot, which vitiates his determination; that one will not compromise; the other dwells overmuch on the faults he finds with whatever doesn't meet his ideals.

In my own case, I didn't care enough. I cared very much about my profession and career, the financial success of my projects and the efficient operation and good name of the firms and institutions I worked for, both out of personal pride and for the happiness and continued employment of my colleagues, and I sought to learn and advance as far as I could. But success requires single-minded devotion and my eight to five was not my only interest.

A notion to ignore: Grit your teeth, put your interests aside and work like a maniac while you're young to make a fortune or build a business which you can live on for the rest of your life while you do what you really want to do. How likely is it that you will be the one out of ten thousand small town boys who goes to Harvard and becomes CEO of General Electric? Or writes an algorithm that conquers Wall Street? The system is rigged, my dears—it ain't gonna happen to you.

How to Survive at Work

Look busy.

How to Succeed to the Extent That Success is Possible

Do your job well. Let people know what you're doing and let them know you're doing it well. Do this without boasting.

Let people know who is fucking up. The trick is doing this without being thought a backstabber. And the fucker upper ain't gonna like it when it gets back to him.

Be cheerful. Your attitude affects other people's attitudes. When you're nervous and hide behind a grave face, they close up too. Smile, and they smile.

Avoid innuendo, don't gossip, don't say bad things about anyone.

Don't play games. Take what people say at face value—assume they mean what they say and say what they mean; act as if they're rational and reasonable.

You can pretend to do a silly task though you actually don't. But be aware that though some bosses forget what they asked you to do, some remember. Go slow until you know which type you're dealing with.

Be fair and equitable.

Have trust and confidence.

Use logic and common sense.

Be patient and respectful.
Show up on time.
Act like nothing is more important than your job.

And Finally

Forty years of honest, solid work and then get laid off. Can't get unemployment compensation, either. At least now I have time to finish a book.

Finding a Job

Grunt Work

My first pay began in the fourth grade as a weekly allowance of twenty-five cents, and when each of my younger sisters and brothers reached the age of ten they received the same. It rose to fifty cents in high school. It wasn't tied to performance of chores as other kids' allowances were; we were expected to do them as a matter of course. Our parents never explicitly said why they gave it to us, though my dad once mentioned that going to school was our job. My allowance was less than what some kids got but I was content with it and happy knowing that I could count on it.

When you're a child you do what's expected because you don't know there's the possibility of doing something else. School was fun. I was good at it and liked learning new things. I liked the praise I got from the teachers and other kids. Since I was the youngest and smallest, I was always last to be chosen for a team on the playground, but I was the best in the classroom.

At eleven I got my first paying job delivering a weekly advertising flyer after school. What a pleasure it was to walk in the rain down the hill from my last stop and build dams in the ditch beside the dirt road until dusk, then dash across the four-lane highway, cross the railroad tracks at the bottom of a cut and arrive home. We moved away shortly after I got the job, though.

My oldest sister and I harvested our cherry tree and sold small bagfuls door to door for a dime. People probably had their own cherries but most were kind enough to buy. Thirty-five years later my wife and I visited that town and as we walked along the sidewalk two tykes on bicycles veered

toward us and skidded to a stop. The older boy dug into his
pockets and offered pebbles for a quarter each. I chose the
most colorful and gave him fifty cents.

I applied for a morning paper route and finally got one,
but only a month later my father was transferred. I put my
name on a new list. There were plenty of routes but there were
also plenty of kids with younger brothers to take them over.
Finally a fellow who was starting a neighborhood paper met
with me and my parents and, impressed with my curriculum
vitae, gave me his first route and a month later a bronze statue
with the inscription *Paperboy of the Month*. Darned if we didn't
move away the next month. After another year on a list I got
another route.

Paper routes were fun in those days. You rode around on
a bike tossing papers, big ones and skinny ones, overhand,
underhand, sidehand, a trick for each house. From the sidewalk you'd sling one over a railing to slide across the porch
and stop at the doormat, walk another end over end up the
stairs, or skitter one around a corner. You could ride no hands
and roll and fling through the warm evening air under a rising full moon, and if you finished early enough you rode a
little further to the airport and leaned against your bike to
watch the airplane fly in overhead.

Once a month you stopped to collect. People paid you
their two-eighty and sometimes they said to keep the change.
If no one was home you stopped next time, and sometimes
you had to make a special weekend trip. Now and then some
deadbeat never paid and you stopped delivering. You were
out your fifty cents, but the newspaper company absorbed
the two-thirty.

These days kids don't deliver papers. Deliverymen drive
a pickup around at four in the morning and you mail your
check to a collection company. Alas.

During my senior year I turned sixteen, got a driver's license and began wearing contact lenses instead of glasses.
The popular kids took me to woodsies with bonfires and beer

and couples necking in the dark. Poor kids—they got pregnant and married, died in drunken car wrecks, and lived out their lives in that small ranching town. At the end-of-year senior assembly they voted me the recipient of a college scholarship whose benefactor had stipulated that the graduating class select from among the top five students. Six hundred forty dollars a year it was, and my parents matched it, and that was almost enough for tuition, books, room and board. Here, kids, wherever you are now, take this book as thanks.

The summer after my first year I couldn't find work until August when the employment office called to offer a job as rodman for a surveyor working out by the airport. He was a kind man who tried to teach me how to calculate angles and distances, but I had just flunked second-semester calculus because I didn't go to the eight o'clock class, having been up too late the night before smoking pot and talking about literature and revolution with people who treated me as an equal despite my age; my pride in my mathematical ability was injured and I wanted nothing to do with it. I'd begun as a math major, but an introductory humanities course opened my eyes to a world I'd barely known existed. Western music, art and literature from Greece to the Romantics, my god! What a revelation! And French and poetry and philosophy! And Renan, *Stranger in a Strange Land,* Frederick Douglass, Malcolm X, and student activism and the occupation of Regent Hall! Math couldn't compare.

The employment office was the place anybody who had a job and no one to do it left word and anybody who wanted a job left his name. My second summer they called with a job clearing trails for the Forest Service. The crew was me, a ranch boy I'd known slightly in high school, and a professor from some eastern college who stayed in a small house trailer with his wife and two grade-school daughters for their summer vacation in the Rockies.

Monday mornings the district ranger drove me and Dwayne to the camp in the hills. The professor met us and we headed up a trail with shovels and a chain saw to where we'd left off Friday. Then we walked until the trail was obstructed, cut branches and downed trees, removed rocks, relevelled the grade, and continued on up. Nights Dwayne and I shared a tent and cooked on a shepherds stove, a metal box over a wood fire that served as an oven whose top was a cooking surface. We spent two weeks building and repairing fish dams in a small creek. A fish dam is a wall of rocks beneath the surface that gives trout a place to hide. At the older dams we would put a hand into a crack, feeling for a tailfin, and if we were quick enough, grab and toss it onto the bank for dinner. The professor and his wife were enthusiastic about my upcoming year at the University of Bordeaux. Dwayne wasn't part of this world, but we developed a certain camaraderie. Friday afternoons the ranger came and drove us back to town.

Off to France in September, the year after the 68 uprising, denunciations of American imperialism, 'pataphysics, the Situationists, Switzerland, Germany, Spain, Morocco—congratulations American you put a man on the moon, thank you but it wasn't me—Nietzsche and colonialism taught by Marxists, Neanderthal caves, poems and music and wine and food, African students—you're a Nixon baby, they sneered. But I'm not, that wasn't me—the invasion of Cambodia, girls and jeunes filles, movies and books, London on the way home.

Back to the Colorado mountains, the Forest Service and Dwayne, but now the boss was a rancher who needed to pick up some income, a bitter middle-aged redneck who held my year abroad against me. The only young men who left America, hell, who left Colorado to go anywhere but Utah or Wyoming were soldiers, and they only left because they were ordered to, and they took care of the gooks and the spics and came home when they were done, glad to be back and shake off the stink. I said I'd visited a hometown boy on the base in Munich, but it didn't help. He and Dwayne became pals right away and stopped waking me up in the morning. I'd pull on my clothes fast when I heard them loading the pickup and they'd look disappointed, and we'd drive off from the busy campground where we were staying and clear trail until mid-afternoon and then go back to empty trashcans for the tourists. The next week they got up earlier and were quieter and left me behind. Over the weekend the ranger called and said he was sorry things hadn't worked out and that I wouldn't be going back. I guess I should have bought an alarm clock the first weekend but it probably wouldn't have made much difference.

After a while the employment office called with a job at the golf course. It was watered between ten at night and six in the morning. Every two hours you moved the sprinklers to new spots, which meant you couldn't sleep, which shot your day all to heck, and it got chilly out there, too. The boss soon called me in, peeved at having to water the spots I'd missed. How can you tell? I asked. They're dry, he said, and fired me. But I still feel bad about letting him down.

The summer's income was so low that I ran out of money my last semester and worked part-time at Kentucky Fried Chicken. In the back room we transferred chicken pieces from boxes of ice to boiling oil, set the timer, added water to powdered potatoes, cleaned spills, ladled coleslaw from large to small containers, put biscuits in the oven, set the timer, wiped up oil. Everything was coated in oil. The permanent employees looked forward to a nickel an hour raise and maybe becoming a manager one day. I scorned the nickel an hour, but over a year it would come to a month's rent and if you're unskilled and uneducated there are worse things than managing a greasy spoon, though I doubt there were enough customers to support as many franchises as there were would-be managers.

Me, I looked no farther forward than to graduation. It came soon enough with a degree in French, a portfolio of student newspaper articles, and no prospects for using either. Home to the Western Slope and the employment office. They hooked me up with a drugstore owner who needed a clerk. He started a book section and asked me to select a few titles that would appeal to the town's youth. I didn't have much latitude because the distributor filled the racks with books that dismayed me but I suppose he knew would sell. I was able to order some Dostoevsky, which probably didn't, and Abbie Hoffman's *Steal This Book,* which greatly displeased the owner because he thought somebody would. To prove him wrong I asked my friends to buy copies but only a couple did. Sorry, owner.

In the fall I helped my family move to a suburb of Denver. I went back to Boulder and found a job in a small factory where they wrapped wires around nails on a sheet of plywood, zipped them together with tie straps, took the bundled wire off the nails and sent it on to another factory for installation in washing machines. We were paid hourly with a bonus for piecework over our quota. My boss spoke highly of the extra quarter I could make, but the boredom killed me and I quit before I even got up to speed. I was broke and so far from knowing what to do with myself that I thought about joining the Navy despite having laid groundwork for a medical draft deferral.

My high school friend Tom, an older high school kid Harry, and Tom's college friend Mike had moved to a mostly abandoned town down the road from Telluride named Placerville, where they rented houses for fifteen dollars a month. I took the few dollars I'd saved and moved in with Tom. We all agreed we'd never sell out and work for The Man, never repeat what successful people said and begin believing what we repeated, never become someone who embodied Wealth's values, become the Wealthy without the wealth, become a sucker. The three of them worked in the mine at Telluride. They went underground before dawn and came out after nightfall talking of drifts and stopes. I applied but wasn't hired because I'd passed part of my draft physical and they didn't want me going off to Vietnam. Nor did I, but I did need a job. I had to leave after a month.

Back to Denver to stay with my parents. I'd been writing poems and stories and songs with Mike and Harry and decided that becoming a journalist would be a step toward the book I told them I was going to write one day, the novel of our generation, which would win me the Nobel and have girls hanging on me, so I applied for a job with The Denver Post, banking on my portfolio of student newspaper articles. They gave me a job delivering advertising proofs to businesses on the west side of town, not what I had in mind but I thought maybe I could move to the editorial side. It was like being a paperboy, not too bad, but without the charm of the bicycle.

I worked there eight months while the Selective Service System gave me another physical and investigated my claim of involvement with the Communist Party in Bordeaux. Meanwhile a fellow from a small town up the river from Bordeaux arranged for me to harvest grapes with a family there. He mentioned that a man from the French intelligence service had asked him if I was a Communist. He'd denied it, to my chagrin.

In June I had an interview with a Defense Intelligence Agency man at the draft center who looked at my yellow and green hair and my dossier and sighed and said, "There's nothing wrong with you."

I shrugged.

"But I think you don't want to go and you wouldn't make a good soldier."

I nodded.

"I'm going to recommend an administrative deferral."

"Okay," I said, afraid to say more.

"You can leave now," he said.

That was the only interview I ever had for a job I was trying not to get.

When August came and it was time to leave for France, my draft status was unresolved so I figured I wouldn't return. Just before I left I was given an administrative deferral. The details were erroneous but I didn't point that out.

Picking grapes is back-breaking, stooping or squatting and clipping and placing the warm plump bunches of grapes into a bucket and taking it full to a 250 liter barrel at the end of the row under the clear blue sky overlooking a valley of golden vineyards under the clear blue sky, amid banter among the crew, who'd grown up together, while M. Baudet recounted the neighborhood goings on and life under the Germans during the war. At ten we took a break. The others drank water but forced wine on me, so I was tipsy until noon when I went to my friend's house in town where I sat with his family at lunch with wine, then back to the vineyard until the four o'clock break with more wine. At five we loaded the barrels on the wagon and the tractor pulled it to the shed where we dumped them into a concrete vat and then sat and drank an aperitif relaxing and chatting and watching the river flow, then a walk to my friend's and dinner with wine and a pousse-café and then to bed. The weekly pay was 200 francs (40 dollars) and two bottles of red or another 10 francs if I didn't want the wine.

Some weekends I visited my sister who was spending her own junior year in Bordeaux. Those weeks I took my two bottles and flirted with the girls she knew. After a stretch of mild intoxication for a week and weekend and the following week, I insisted on water during the breaks. M. Baudet insisted.

"But you're all drinking water," I said.

"But you're the American guest," he said.

I was loathe to decline his kindness and hospitality but stood my ground. Forty years later I published his wartime memoirs and learned that the locals took glee in inebriating new harvesters.

In my spare time I wrote poems, prose poems, ideas, ideas for stories. A man opens a funeral parlor and skins the corpses to make lamp shades and belts, his products are sold in fine shops; or it was a funeral parlor for dogs and he made stoles and jackets. A young man dodges the draft by moving to France, picks grapes, gets a job teaching skiing in the Alps, marries a French woman, has a family; or he starts feeling cut off from things, asks if he's going to spend his life bouncing from one temporary job to another, craves a serious and enduring vocation, decides to become a doctor, throws up the skiing job, heads for home via Morocco and a visit to a friend in the Canary Islands, a spider in a frying pan, running madly round, lifting his feet to give the pain some relief, no escape, at the controls of a mechanical eighteen-legged monster run berserk, fighting with wrenching levers and wheels, casting quick anxious glances at the dials or out the portholes at searing flames, riding the controls like a buck dog with pepper up its ass, trying to balance the flux, slow the insanity, resynchronize the calibrations, ergs squiggling past the windshield, giant footsteps in the air around, turbulence, a huge fingernail reaching down to draw indecipherable in-structions on the sand the clouds the waves.

In Boulder I talked to the dean of med school admissions. My French degree was worthless. I should work on a masters degree while I picked up the pre-med requirements in order to apply. He recommended grad work in a field I liked so if I didn't get in I'd have something to fall back on. But what to study? Marine biology, extraterrestrial biology, genetics? I talked to the nursing school, who said I could apply with my degree but only for the year after next.

I was restless. Spent a night with Mike and a couple other guys, comfortable surrounded by friends and the restless-ness not as stark as it had been in France. I was jumping in more than one direction at once, being pulled many ways, and wanted to take all the paths. I felt like I should be doing something else. I always felt like that when the newness of a situation wore off. I was a big phony. I had friends in grad school, artists, poets, historians, smart and accomplished people, but I excelled at nothing, was merely good enough at everything to make everyone think I was great at everything (people were easy to fool). Friends who were in fact great told me I had the potential for anything but hadn't begun yet. It was good to hear that—maybe I could do as well as they had.

I went to Placerville, then back to Denver for Christmas. My father, two or three sisters and a brother drove me back to Placerville and left with the impression that I was wasting my time and accomplishing nothing. I struggled against the sense of responsibility my father had instilled. I had a little money and moved in with Tom. Mike was in Denver but Harry and his girlfriend Nancy were there. Tom left for Denver; he told me later I'd driven him crazy. Harry and Nancy did carpentry when they could. Harry played guitar, Nancy brooded, and later she killed herself.

Now and then I'd get a ride to Montrose and visit my high school history teacher, who encouraged me to get serious and write a book instead of talk about it, so over the winter I read Proust in French so as not to influence my style and worked hours each day on what I planned to be a best-selling novel about a naïve young American putting together a hashish deal in Morocco. Three months later I gave the product to my teacher.

A week later he poured me a glass of scotch and said, "Jack, it stinks. What do you know about drug deals and Morocco? Write about something you know. Write about family life—you have a good family. There aren't any stories about good families."

He was right about the novel, but I didn't know what to say about good families and I couldn't imagine becoming the next Miller or Céline by writing about families.

I was out of money in the spring. Back to Boulder. Thanks to a high school friend who now booked the acts at the Skunk Kreek Inn, a sophomoric pickup joint that only served beer, I got a job as doorman a couple nights a week. Its clientele was high school kids and university students too young for the bars that served hard liquor. The bands were local groups and occasionally lesser-known national bands; the house favorite was a soul group from Boulder who played in Vegas and LA and Chicago, but they were never away for long because their most ardent audiences were at the Drunk Skunk. It was lousy music but everybody thought it was great because everybody else did.

There was a waitress named Candi, another named Mary Beth, and a bouncer named Rick. The girls hung around with pseudo football players; they weren't quite in the league of their sorority sisters who slept with real ones. They liked being the object of desire, but wouldn't put out when it came down to it, the type who goes to bed with a guy but keeps her clothes on all night. Rick lived with a couple ex-football players, lifted weights, laughed a lot and drank a lot of beer. I worked there because I wanted to get laid. There was a certain prestige in working there but it never did me much good. Rick was there for the same reason and had better luck.

I found a fulltime job managing a private swimming pool ten hours a day six days a week for the princely sum of three hundred dollars a month for a guy who ran four or five pools. I soon felt that I was being taken advantage of and I didn't like the clientele, inhabitants of $25,000 condominiums who were snooty about their private pool. I had a hard time getting up in the morning to watch their kids play and measure water chemistry after nights at the Skunk. The Skunk gave me a check every two weeks with tax and social security deducted, no deduction for medical premiums because there was no insurance. The pool guy gave me cash and after two weeks asked if I'd take a personal check. I'd rather have cash, I said, trusting the real thing more than his check. Then he asked me to close up the pool in the evening since he had too many to do himself. I said okay, except for the nights I have my other job. I taught the two girl guards how to do it so I could leave a little early, which wasn't really taking advantage of them because their parents didn't pick them up until closing time anyway.

At the Skunk I sat in the vestibule and checked people's wrists as they came in to be sure they'd paid. If they hadn't I'd tell them they needed to, and if they objected I'd look at Rick and he'd have a talk with them. It was boring as hell, making me deaf, poisoning my system, giving me headaches, making me sleep late and rot, and at the pool I sat on a chair for hours trying to stay awake. I decided to quit and find some honest work, get up earlier and eat like a horse.

Job Search
(Down and Out in Boulder and Denver)

Spent much of the day running around, walking around on my feet, searching for food or a job or the money owed me for my last three days at the swimming pool. Like the character in *Hunger* I don't like to bring up the subject of how hungry I am and how much I need a job. I go to D&G's on the pretext of returning a book but really to ask D if he's found me a job where he works, then to O&R's for dinner after which they take me to the Drunk Skunk to ask Rick about a construction job he mentioned three weeks ago. I was sly, I didn't ask outright, only asked how things were going, and he said he hadn't talked to the guy yet and he was getting pissed off because the guy owed him five hundred dollars for the car he bought, and one of these days he's gonna go over and kill him, which he could easily do, his biceps are as big as my thighs, and he's looking for a job himself, so no luck for me, and I walk back to my place.

I have the phone numbers of the two lifeguards and go upstairs to ask Val if I can use her telephone but she isn't there, the door is locked, and the only people I can think of to use their phone are D&G and O&R so I walk to D&G's but the lights are out so I head for O&R's thinking in each of these houses is a telephone but you can't just go up and knock and ask, "Hey, can I use your phone for half an hour?" Nobody's home at O&R's either so I sit on a bench outside thinking hm, what am I gonna do next, maybe I ought to slow down for a minute and think all this over because maybe I don't have to move so fast, I'll starve sooner or later so why not start now; but I really do have to make a couple calls tonight so I don't have to walk around so much tomorrow.

But there's no place with a telephone that I won't be ashamed to ask to borrow so I go home and upstairs to Val's hoping she's there. She is, so I go in and chitchat about this and that for a couple minutes before I ask if she'll let me use the phone, but she never had one put in, so I'm stumped for good. She says go get Jeff the manager to let you in Jim's room and I'm so desperate that I do, saying I'll come back after I make the calls.

Jeff lets me in, and neither of the lifeguards is home but their parents say they got checks today at work so things look good for me. I call the boss's house to deliver my ultimatum which is that if he doesn't mail me the check I'll call the district attorney and the Red Cross to say he's teaching swimming without a certified instructor on staff, and also the state swimming pool chief to say the chlorine levels aren't being checked as often as they should, but he's not there. His wife gives me his office number, which I already have, says call tomorrow; and that's that for the check, should be about twenty-six dollars of which I owe eight to O&R for the money I borrowed for rent.

Then I call J&P to see about a job at J's lumberyard, but I only let the phone ring three times because they are probably in bed. Just long enough to get one of them droopeyed up and stumbling into furniture heading for the phone, a hand on the receiver when the third ring is cut off in the middle, lousy thing to do. At least they won't know I was the one who did it, but that's lousy too.

Okay, now I'll try to find John Bayles and ask about a job driving cabs in Denver, but Information doesn't have his number and I remember that he mentioned when I was there with L (L who used to work with John at the lumberyard when we lived on Maxwell with John and Betsy upstairs) six weeks ago that he couldn't get a phone in his name. (All these bare facts of the evening, dates and places, this is too impersonal, I should write better but it's late at night and I'm compelled to get it all half-assed down.) I can't remember Betsy's last name, probably never knew, and that's that.

Walk out the door trying to remember if there was anyone else I wanted to call while I had the chance, nope, lock the door and see Tina by my room and remember I wanted to call her, well this is much better, my god, we sure came close to missing each other, another example of my fabulous luck.

She takes me out into the dark in her car and we drive along three blocks trying to recognize John's house which I only saw once at night, and do find it but the lights are out, so I go upstairs where they tell me John moved and took Betsy with him and they don't have their address, but wait! Here's a bank statement with Betsy's last name on it so I thank them, and Tina and I find a pay phone, I borrow a dime from her, and Information has the number.

John's at work in Denver but Betsy is encouraging, says talk to him tomorrow; things are better and better, I start grinning, not the clown grin (a hallucination of myself laughing at the cosmic joke) but the everyday pleased with how well things are going grin. We drop by their new place to hand Betsy her bank statement and then on to the Skunk to look for a friend of Tina's to babysit tomorrow while she goes to job interviews.

Friend is not there, we drink a beer and dance to a good band, jazz of the loud snake trees falling rock and recoil type, then drive back to my place. Tina has to pick up her father from work in fifteen minutes so we kiss goodbye and she will bring her daughter over tomorrow at eight and I will babysit.

I did not eat for three days and didn't have a penny so I couldn't make telephone calls. People will give you cigarettes, buy you booze, et cetera, the unnecessaries, but they are stingy when you sheepishly ask for some food because you haven't eaten for two days. Sister and brother-in-law not grudging but looking askance, why don't you get a job [like the rest of us], you can live on two sixty-five an hour and me saying yes of course (what can you do when you're not working, can't even buy paints to portray the beautiful world). Neither of them has ever been broke, tight times sometimes, everybody's in a squeeze now and then, but in their case it's high school to college and a nice decent job at two sixty-five, marriage and the in-laws, ugh, sometimes I can't stand to be around them. I was too proud to ask my parents for help, I was on my own, they had five other kids to support and not a lot to do it with, though it was reassuring to know they were there if I ever really needed them. I walked a lot, that's how things are when you don't have much money, everybody should do it now and then, keep the juices flowing and learn your fellow man. Finally I compromised and told myself I would take anything that paid two fifty, thinking of Tina and her baby, you shouldn't get serious without a bit of bun, a crackerful of crust, a smattering of cash, steady if not phenomenal. But there were no jobs. It was worse than I thought.

Tomorrow: First thing, I will go to the offices of the Denver & Rio Grande Western Railroad. Second, I will go to the offices of Navajo Freight Lines. Third, I will go to the offices of Teamsters Local 17. Fourth, I will bemoan and bewail and curse the dreary repetition of the offices and myself.

And tomorrow: Colorado State Unemployment. The Denver Post, maybe they'll take me back. University of Denver. Adolph Coors, Inc.

And tomorrow I finally lucked out and a guy said we have a crew down in Aurora who I think need some help, it pays five dollars. I was quite pleased that it was so much but when I got the job it paid only three plus overtime. Still, I was lucky to find anything.

I took the bus to Denver and on the way from the station in my dad's car asked if I could borrow it the next day to go to work and said I needed to buy one.

He said, "What for? Cars pollute in a number of ways," which he enumerated.

I said, "Well, how come you've been telling me of so many good deals in the classifieds if you don't want me to get one?" And, "I'm twenty-two, for Pete's sake. How old were you when you got a car?"

He stopped talking and remembered and said, "Sixteen

or seventeen," and didn't say anything after that.

While I ate supper, my first food in days, he looked in the paper and made a couple phone calls and when I finished he said, "Come on, let's go look at some cars."

On the way he said, "Look at all these farts *driving for pleasure.*" I sighed.

We looked at a VW and Dad said to the owner, "I'll give you three fifty." (Fifty dollars less than advertised and twenty-five less than asked.)

Amid wailing from young collegiate wifey sad to see old friend car go after so many years of faithful and rusting service, hubby said, "Done." My participation in the grand sport of bargaining was also done, without a peep.

I drove Dad's car home while he drove the VW, still an adolescent with a new car.

And then to work, forty miles each way, to shovel dirt over a freshly laid sewer pipeline for eleven or twelve hours each day, good hard work down in the solid weighty fact of the earth, the heavy metals elemental, build up your shoulders and tan your arms and redden your neck. Consequent nightmares and sunburned neck, hardening of muscles and deterioration of fingers (were they stretching to accommodate bulging knuckle muscles or had the joints been wrenched apart?). The foreman walked along the top of the ditch and lobbed dirt clods onto our hardhats. I got pissed off and threw one back into his fat belly. He left us alone after that but when the ditch was finished so was I. "Work is a drag," said a guy in the ditch, "and you're paid for being a drag. And they make it as big a drag as they can. Last week I asked for a job it would have been easy to let me have but they didn't give it to me." These are the true and underlying conditions of the working world.

A job as stonemason for ten dollars an hour fell through. I got a job in a machine shop despite the misgivings of the foreman who said college graduates never stayed long, and as it turned out the D&RGW offered me a job a week later. Sorry, foreman. And who knows—crawling into extensible

metal tubes to wipe them down wasn't fun but I might eventually have learned something useful.

My mother's uncle had been an engineer for the CB&Q.
He was kind to us kids and trains were a big deal in the small
Great Plains towns we'd grown up in, so I was well disposed
to working for a railroad. My mother told me later he'd been
a civil engineer. I couldn't be a switchman or a brakeman
because I didn't have 20/20 vision so I became a graveyard
shift clerk standing by as trains came in or walking the yard
taking down car numbers, finding out where they were going and writing that down (four units followed by a C&O
box followed by twenty Q pigs and an SF flat for the lowcar
and Rio Grande caboose 01417 with conductor Subry and
then two helper units, though why did they need six units to
pull a mere 1,400 tons over the mountains? And why for the
life of me was I sitting at the crossing watching that train go
by?—aside from having to wait before I could drive across)
and sending copies on the telex to everybody on the railroad
so they knew where their cars were. I was a paperboy again.
By two AM my lips were frozen and I couldn't talk, though
there wasn't a soul I could talk to anyway unless I wanted
to talk about football or make noisy jokes about what their
wives were doing while they were at work. One guy asked if
I was reading dirty French novels when he saw me reading
Proust. It paid four dollars an hour plus plenty of overtime,
between six fifty and eight hundred a month.

I lived with my parents in Denver, repaid my debts to
them, got an apartment downtown, and revised the Morocco
book at two pages a day until I lost interest. You have to write
for yourself or your friends or the friends you want to have,
not the best-seller list.

I had wonderful insights into the meanings of things, the
genesis of cultural phenomena, the workings of the mind, my
mind, of course, but the processes I observed in myself also
operated in others, good Enlightenment thinking, the prin-
ciple of uniformitarianism, which when applied to rocks, for

example, postulates that the physical processes we observe today also operated in the past and were responsible for the formation of the geologic features we see. I told myself I should be writing what streamed through my mind, at least jotting down the topics of that flow so that I could at leisure, when I found the leisure, collate them, systematize them, make an opus, another treatise of human nature or at least a portrayal of excited youthful thought, but I usually gave up when the thoughts outpaced the act of writing. I told myself that they would keep coming and I could tap them any time, but I knew it wasn't true and that I was letting my inspiration go to waste.

Hume was lucky, he'd had leisure; I had to earn a living. Had I but a day or a week to concentrate instead of an hour or two, I would put aside acrostics, a book a friend suggested, a letter in response, a party where I might meet a girl, and buckle down to transcribing my thoughts wherever they led. But it was not a good excuse. I was indolent, and even Hume must have had to overcome indolence (he had described it well). I procrastinated: I wrote long letters and prose poems, easy stuff, but put off the hard work.

Wallace Stevens was an insurance company executive who wrote poetry—what a wonder!—a businessman who wrote poetry. I was slow to learn that poets need to make a living somehow. I thought artists only artified—they didn't have jobs like the rest of us. I realized much later that though writing may bring fame and even fortune, you have to support yourself along the way.

Samuel Beckett said he wrote in French because it forced him to examine his thoughts and modes of expression. Should I force myself to write in French? "Force" was the operative word. Sometimes I couldn't even force myself to talk. In France it had often been so much effort to express even a single nuanced thought that I would let someone else divine my meaning and then agree yes, that's what I mean. I must have been tedious to be with sometimes, and it wasn't the way to write a book.

But I needed to experience something worth writing about. The writers I admired had lived life, moved around, met interesting people. What had I done? Five years of infancy, sixteen of school and two of odd jobs and travel. Orwell joined the Spanish revolution; I dodged the Vietnam draft. Miller lived in Paris; I picked grapes one season in a village and then scampered home. Tolstoy wrote about unhappy families; I ate dinner with my happy one. Huxley explored psychedelics, Kerouac Buddhism, Koestler scientific thought; I took acid, read Suzuki, and flunked out of calculus. Their lives had been incomparably more interesting than mine.

The search for a companion was a great distraction. If only I could find a woman to live with, the time spent yearning and searching for sexual relief would be freed up and I would write from a base of contentment and domestic harmony. My dad advised, "Marry a smart woman," but the smart women I met weren't cute and sexy, and the ones I found to sleep with didn't share my thoughts, didn't think much at all, weren't interested in literature, were too frivolous for me to imagine spending my life with. I spent a lot of time coping one way or another with my concupiscence.

When I did write I wrote about lack of faith, unhappiness, despair and decadence, which rather romanticized worries about finding a job, dissatisfaction with the one I had, shame about not writing more, and my desperate desire for sex. It was easy to write like Baudelaire but not authentic, I was no denizen of the gutter. But then, was he? Maybe he'd sold insurance too. Whether he had or not, poems like his had been written; mine were imitations. I wrote easily and could write anything I chose, but I had nothing to say. Well, my jottings might serve one day to portray juvenility in a character in some book.

It would have helped to have a market, a publisher, an agent, some chance of having my work read by strangers. But how to find these things? *Writer's Digest's* cheerful admonitions and success stories put me off but they did offer one worthwhile bit of advice—submit a piece again and again. I never thought I had a piece good enough to submit in the first place. I should have submitted anyway, submitted anything.

After seven months with the railroad I'd saved two thousand dollars and decided to get serious about writing a new novel. I would hitchhike to San Francisco, visit Tom and Mike and then head south via train and bus to Mexico, then El Salvador where my history teacher knew someone, through Central America and northern South America to French Guiana where I knew someone, and then down the eastern coast to Sao Paulo where someone else had a friend. There I would find an apartment and hole up and write.

I saw sights in Mexico City for a couple days, took a tour agent to a movie, heard from some Americans that Costa Rica was a good place to go, was too impatient to take the train and flew straight to San Jose, heard the Pacific coast was a good place to go, flew to Quepos where I met an exiled Argentine journalist and his Colombian girlfriend who invited me to stay with them in San Jose. They eked out a living by her making empañadas for a vendor, always singing, happy to be with him, while he typed in the living room. I stayed in my room studying Spanish and reading and writing letters about my impressions and my aim to write books, each book a contribution to the body of thought and beauty created by the best minds across the centuries, or failing that, to make my life a work of art (perhaps a nobler goal). What would be a life lived artfully? Each moment a pearl on the string that was myself within the harmonious weave of nature, each instant savored so that what remained of life no matter how long or short would be dessert, an unnecessary but delightful prolonging of repletion, of partaking in this dinner spread before us all... Until she very kindly told me that they were worried about me holed up in my room and I should get out more. So I took a train to the Caribbean for a week, snorkeled, played checkers with the local kids, and returned thinking I should move on to Brazil. The Argentine told me that Buenos Aires was more cosmopolitan than

Brazil so I decided to go there. The girlfriend asked me to deliver a letter to her twin sister in Bogota since their parents would intercept it if it came in the mail. I flew to Isla de San Andres which I heard was a good place to snorkel, stayed in the poor part of town away from the casinos, skin dived from a motorboat, got a haircut. By now my frame of reference had shifted as usual when I travelled on my own to one based on acceleration and I moved pretty fast, flew to Cartagena, saw the castle, was cheated by sleight of hand exchanging currency on the street, flew to Bogota, delivered the letter to the very kind and appreciative sister happy for news of her eloped twin, a short hour in their parents' house in a gated community with the taxi waiting outside while she read the letter and thanked me and gave me tea and cookies, back to the city, robbed at knifepoint, the bandits shot at by a man in a suit as they ran down the hill—should I run away before he comes back to shoot me?—a plainclothed cop who told me to file a complaint at the police station, maybe my money would be recovered, was called in for a lineup of six men being beaten with a rubber truncheon, identified one of them as one of the bandits, what happened to him? did he go to prison? as the feeling of rootlessness set in, running out of money, better get back to the US of A before I'm flat broke, flew to Miami, found a driveaway car to Alabama where I realized I was totally free and was squandering my freedom and freedom meant the capacity to get engaged in anything I wanted, so after I delivered my presents to my family in Denver I would go live in San Francisco and get engaged, find a profession, develop my talents, anyway some of them because they can't all be developed, didn't matter which, just develop something, become accomplished at something, hitchhiked from Alabama to Denver, got another driveaway car to transport my things, arrived in SF where Tom and Mike put me up, had to find a job, make some money.

More Clerking

A temporary agency sent me to Standard Oil as a teletype operator where we sent telexes all over the world instructing ships where to take their cargos. The lady next to me asks, "Where's Muscat?"

I point to the map and say, "Here."

"What country is that in?" she asks and I say, "United Arab Emirates."

She asks, "What country is Dubai in?"

"It's one of the Trucial States." I don't quite know what that is either but we send ten messages a day there.

She mulls. "Where is the United Arab Republic?"

I point and say, "Here. They changed the name. It used to be Egypt."

"Oh." Then she says, "I thought... You know, they used to say Cairo, Egypt."

"Yeah," I say. "Now they say Cairo, United Arab Republic."

The dust settles on that. Then she says, "I wonder if the Egyptians like the Arabs?"

Another guy's talking about somebody whose name he can't remember. "You know, a good poet, that poet laureate, what's his name?"

"Poet laureate of where?" I ask.

"Robert Frost, that's who it is. He's a good poet, a great poet. He's the best, the best poet there is."

I don't get a chance to say anything while he rattles on but finally I say I don't like Frost.

"What? He's the best American poet there ever was. Why don't you like him?"

Now look, I don't care. Somebody likes Frost, that's okay.

I don't say anything.

He presses the issue. "Frost talks about the basics, the earth, America. How can you not like him?"

"I just don't care for him," I say, hoping he'll give up on me.

"Listen," he says. "I'll tell you what it is. I'll tell you why you don't like Frost. Don't get upset at me. There's a deep reason why you don't like him."

"Tell me."

"You're prejudiced."

A while later he says, "You know Van Gogh, the painter?"

"Yeah."

"I'll bet you don't like him either."

The lady next to me says I should apply for a permanent clerical position. I ask my boss about it and she suggests taking some filing classes at the community college and then talking to her. Right, a class to learn the alphabet. Forget it.

I had taken the civil service test and the IRS hired me. At a gray metal desk in a huge windowless room with dozens of people at other gray metal desks I took a paper-clipped tax return from a stack on the left, put the clip in a bowl, piled some of the papers at top center, stapled the rest and placed them on a pile on the right, and reached for the next. By afternoon I wondered how long this would go on and next morning I wondered if it was a psychological test and if I didn't crack I'd be given something else to do. A couple young colleagues invited me to the cafeteria for lunch where they talked about their aspirations to become auditors. It seemed that was the cushy job. That afternoon I was sure it was a test, and if I passed I'd be on the path to auditordom. After a night's sleep I realized it was not a test and mid-morning asked my supervisor if there was something else I could do. She said that if after a couple months she saw that I'd learned the ins and outs of the job, she would consider giving me some new tasks. I had lunch with the aspirants again and then quit.

What do you do when you're in a lousy job and can't see a hope of improvement? They say to vote with your feet. Fine, that may work for shoppers—if people stop buying a crummy product, the vendor is either going to improve it or go out of business—but walking away from a job isn't going to improve conditions for the others or for the new guy who takes your spot. Though it could if everyone quit... But they won't.

You can go to work and pretend you're not there, learn the tricks of dumbing and numbing yourself so you don't notice time pass until you can leave for the day. But then you're trapped. You can't look for another job when you're working all day, and you become dumb and numb.

Or you can refuse to continue, and quit. It's a personal choice, a question of taste. But when you quit you start going broke. Me, I tended to quit.

Choosing a Profession

I was lucky that time. A lady I met in a bar had also spent a year in France, and she said the engineering company she worked for had a project in Zaire and they might need a French speaker. Since I also knew how to operate a telex, they hired me as typist for this new-fangled word processing machine they had. I typed specifications on an IBM Selectric with a memory device that coded the text using software called APL. At 4:30 each day I hit a switch that connected the device to an IBM 360 computer at a service company in Los Angeles. The material was printed and trucked by courier to arrive at my office the next morning.

It was a decent job. The engineers had a broader outlook than construction laborers, railroad clerks, telex operators and auditor wannabes. My boss was French, there was a young French engineer, and the American secretary of the Zairois representative in the office was bilingual. A lively group of young people had drinks after work.

I took advantage of the word processor to print my poetry. I sent a piece on nocturnal life in the city to a local weekly and received a very kind and encouraging rejection from the literary editor. I read poems at the Intersection in North Beach, and a well-known beat poet asked if I'd be interested in arranging his papers. You bet! Get to know the guy, meet his friends, see unpublished stuff, read correspondence, learn about the life behind the City Lights circle, Ferlinghetti, Ginsberg, Kerouac, my entrée to the world of the accomplished and famous! We made a date, he opened the door and showed me around his dingy flat making nervous chitchat. He was very nervous. I finally asked him to show me the material he

wanted me to work on. Two measly shoeboxes on the floor
of his bedroom, and then he asked me to go to bed. Maybe
I would have despite my strong orientation to women, but
he was unshaven and smelly. No thanks, I said, I'm sorry,
goodbye; and thus ended my brush with the beat generation.

My Colorado friends and I read a lot and talked a lot.
They talked about what we read and I talked about what I
was going to write. Mike and I wrote songs we played on the
guitar. Tom and I played chess and talked about society and
the perfectibility of humankind. The group expanded. Manny
from Nebraska and Bordeaux moved to San Francisco and
worked on a book. Tom's sister Kathy moved to San Francisco and wrote stories and taught ESL. Tom's cousin George
organized a Hegel discussion group. Manny and Kathy got
everyone involved in a play they wrote called *Godzilla Meets
Anthony and Cleopatra,* but I dropped out because I didn't want
to collaborate—I wanted full control over my creations. They
played at the Intersection and were reviewed in *The Chronicle,*
though alas they were panned.

The bilingual secretary and I hit it off. She read books
from the classical canon and we had good discussions about
literature although she wasn't excited by the beats or dada
or OULIMPO. She liked music, the symphony, the opera;
her family was from the old stock that supports them. When
I was dumped by an artsy ex-nurse poet, she invited me to
Thanksgiving with her family. She was good, kind, generous,
concerned to do the right thing, the respectable thing, ab-
horred the wrong, concurred with my work ethic and moral
outlook and helped to focus it on volunteer work and criticism
of wrong action and evil-doers. This is good for a person and
good for society, though it may hamper a novelist trying to
describe human nature. We got engaged.

JFDP, the company we worked for, sent me around the
country twice to interpret for visiting Zairois representatives.
We saw a railroad car manufacturing plant in Idaho, flew a
helicopter in Colorado, wined and dined at the Ex-Im Bank in
DC and Chase Bank in New York. JFDP was an engineering

subsidiary of a very large construction company with international civil works projects and many defense contracts. The local executives were mostly ex-military men. Despite my aversion to the military-industrial complex, engineering began to look like a decent way to make a living. The engineers had stable jobs and earned enough to raise families, and the work of designing things to be built seemed constructive. So I got engaged again—I applied to engineering school.

We got married, she worked fulltime at JFDP, I went to school, worked holidays and vacations at JFDP, did homework, didn't write, rejoined family life—mostly hers because it was nearby, sometimes mine—from family to family I had moved with a bit of bohemian interregnum, it probably boiled down to lack of belief that I could actually succeed at writing, and I didn't really want to be a homosexual drug-taking beatnik, either, when it came to it. It turned out she wasn't as enthusiastic about mating as I was, so I didn't have quite the marital contentment I'd envisioned, but nothing's perfect. She was a good person and eventually we had good kids and a good family. And I felt I that wasn't wasting my time, I was accomplishing something, and I would write again later.

I had to choose a concentration within engineering. Since I was keen on alternative energy sources, particularly solar, the mechanical courses which included thermodynamics and energy conversion seemed the most promising. For my senior project I designed a residential solar hot water heating system, which in those days only back-to-nature communal types talked about. Thirty years later it's catching on.

One of my professors encouraged me to do graduate work in applied math. I was tempted, but seven years of college was enough, and I wanted to work in the real world, and it was only fair for me to put my wife through school to finish her bachelor's degree.

The APL software salesman/programmer who developed reports showed me how to do it, and soon it was faster to write the code myself than wait for him. One Christmas I spent a few hours writing a program to summarize the answers to an office questionnaire. The human resources director was mightily impressed and made sure I kept my part-time job. Then during my last semester the salesman offered me a job with his company. The pay was good and it would start immediately. They flew me to LA to meet the owner in some office park housing the staff and computers. The owner wore polyester slacks and white shoes, took me to lunch, talked a blue streak about their growth and customers and my rosy future and how they needed me at once and couldn't wait for me to finish my degree. Back in SF I politely declined.

"I want to finish my engineering degree," I said.

"But you don't need it for this," the salesman said.

"I'm so close," I said, "and I've worked almost three years on it. I want it so I'll always have something to fall back on."

"You'll make more money at this than engineering," he said.

I knew he was probably right, but there was something else and since by then we were friends I told him. "He wore white shoes." He didn't understand, and I saw that our values differed so I didn't explain that it was too suburban for my taste, too ephemeral, not solid like engineering.

Two months later I had another degree and I'd passed the Engineer-In-Training exam, the prerequisite for taking the Professional Engineer exam after two years of work experience.

JFDP offered a position, of course. Though they'd been kind to us, I'd been interested to see what was available and had applied elsewhere, too. Actually it was the HR fellow who'd been kind. JFDP was the most recent in a string of temporary jobs but now I was starting a professional career—my next job would be the first of a new string and it was important to start well. I did consider their projects around the world, but we wouldn't be living abroad for a while as there was my wife's BA to get through. As it came to pass, the parent company felt no more loyalty to them than I did—they shut the place down a couple years later and laid everyone off.

I interviewed with the gas and electric company, but they acted like they would be doing me a favor by hiring me and told me they expected their employees to serve on community organization boards in their spare time, and I decided that I didn't want their monopoly extending over my personal life.

NASA offered a job as a facilities design engineer, and they did exciting things like space travel, experimental aircraft and extraterrestrial ecology, and furthermore my father had always worked for the government, and his father for the Post Office, so I'd be following their footsteps into the public sector. My dad had told me as a child that he thought working for the government was working for the people of the country. I chose NASA.

Learning the Job

Public Sector I :
Bafflement

It turned out that what I did at NASA was design building systems—heating, ventilating and air conditioning, lighting and power—nothing glamorous. They did, though, have an arrangement with Stanford for their employees to take classes toward a master's degree, tuition paid with leave during the workweek for one class each quarter. I enrolled in a dynamics class but the math was beyond me and I didn't see how to assimilate a year's worth of math to keep up, so I dropped it; thus ended my academic career.

People at work were very relaxed. There was little pressure to meet deadlines, though maybe they didn't expect much from me because I was young and green. On the other hand, there was no guidance and I didn't know who to go to with questions; I wasn't even sure who was my boss. I carefully designed a support to hold models in a small wind tunnel and following the guidance of a book on drafting loaned by a fellow employee produced a set of drawings whose equal I never saw. I thought that's what you were supposed to do. The drawings left my desk and some months later I had a call from a machine shop saying their product missed my specifications by a couple thousandths of an inch and asking if that was okay or if they should try again. I had no idea. I found the name of the researcher who'd wanted the support in the first place and called him to ask. He said it didn't matter.

A group played soccer at lunchtime twice a week and other days I joined another group to jog around the field. Some afternoons when I had nothing to do I'd get on a bike and ride out to watch the U-2s take off or land.

I had no idea what was going on around me or where I fit in. The forty-mile commute was awful so we moved to the South Bay, but the traffic was even worse and we moved back to the city. A year passed. I got tired of feeling lost and thought I was wasting my time so I found a job in the city.

PRIVATE SECTOR I :
LEARNING

Cadwell Engineers was a small consulting firm run by a man whose father had started it and whose son would take it over. There were a bunch of cranky old engineers and a few young people. I was lucky to have a great boss, Larry, who told me what to do and how and why and then checked my work to make sure I'd understood. We designed building systems, not particularly exciting, but I learned how to size ductwork and piping, select equipment, draft with my tie tucked into my shirt, write specifications, and complete the construction documents that told the contractor what to build.

One of the cranky old men, impatient with my slow assembly of a set of drawings, grabbed them to show me how to hold them by one corner while putting them in order and then roll them face-side out so that when unrolled they didn't curl off the table. There was a lot to learn and I took my learning where I could.

The worst old man was grumpy, picky, sarcastic, impossible to please, a constant torment, but he did have the decency to kill himself one weekend. All assholes should do that.

Larry left for a firm which had offered him a partnership and he told me, "You should come to Haravan. There's a future there, not like this place where you'll work for the family the rest of your life."

PRIVATE SECTOR II :
ENGINEERING

I took his advice and went, though after a few years I found that the future at Haravan & Associates had ended with him. The other four partners weren't inclined to expand the ownership.

One of them didn't like me at all. Nor I him, which began during my interview when Ernie asked when I could start.

"My wife's due to have a baby any day now," I said. "What if we say two weeks after that?"

His lips pursed. "I don't know. I think Larry needs you right now. You'll have to talk to him."

So I did. "Sure," said Larry. "Just call when you're ready."

Reminds me of another interview years later. My prospective boss asked, "Can you start January second?"

"I could," I said, "but my mother is very ill and we kids decided she shouldn't have too many visitors at once, so we've scheduled our visits to her in New Mexico. Mine is the first week of January. Would you mind if I start the ninth?"

Pursed lips. "I would really like to shift this project over to you so I can get back to my other work."

"Well, let me see if I can arrange to go the week before Christmas." But I didn't. Fuck heartless people. I turned down the job.

This one I took because Larry was such a good guy.

Ernie was not. He couldn't stand to be wrong about anything, couldn't stand thinking that anyone might be as competent as he, had to have the last word, and was very defensive. As a last resort, he would lie about something he'd said or done if he later felt it showed him in poor light. He was stingy and found fault with experienced engineers but was generous and protective of the young graduates he hired and mentored—as long as they deferred to his wisdom and knowledge.

He'd sold air conditioning equipment before he became a consulting engineer. Salesmen and liars, always watching, gauging your reaction, calculating their influence. It's more important to appear to be than to be, more important to win even than to profit. He listened to himself for so long that he ended up believing his own bullshit. With clients he pretended to be familiar with all the details of a job, but he seldom talked with his designers beforehand, so the clients left with different messages: the accurate one they'd earlier received from a designer and Ernie's contradictory assertion. Then he spoke contemptuously of their confusion.

Engineering is about making things work and in the end it doesn't matter what you say—either they work or they don't. I was surprised to learn that no one checked systems after installation to make sure they worked as intended. It was in no one's scope and no one was paid to do it. (This is changing. Now it's more common to include what's known as commissioning.) At the end of a project, when the fee was expended and the equipment was running and the occupants had occupied, the engineer was the first to be called when problems arose. Ernie's projects had no problems. If he couldn't convince the client that it wasn't a problem at all, he put them off with promises to call in the installer or vendor or manufacturer to fix it, and to call in another when the last couldn't, until whoever was complaining gave up. End of problem.

One day Ernie asked me and a colleague, another ex-salesman who wanted to design, why we hadn't submitted a proposal for a certain project.

"Because you said you don't want Haravan doing condominiums," I said.

"I never said that," he said.

When we left his office the other guy said, "But he told us that last week, didn't he?" He left soon, disappointed by the fraud.

I stayed on, since I didn't have to work only with Ernie. Larry believed in honest work and taught me how to do it. He felt that the best sales strategy was building a reputation for doing a good job, which jibed with me. He enjoyed lunch now and then with a client or a contractor or equipment representative and often brought me along. People those days drank hard liquor until the food arrived and then drank wine. I don't know how Larry accomplished anything afterwards— I couldn't.

I passed the professional mechanical engineer exam and was licensed by the state. Hooray! The end of schooling and tests!

They made me an associate to enhance my prestige with clients and staff and assure me that I was on the track to partnership. The honor included breakfast with the principals once a month and it meant that I had to tell other people what to do for the first time in my life. I was a boss. I worried about how to do it right, if I seemed to know what I was doing, whether the designers and drafters liked me. Then I decided to ignore how I might appear and just give orders politely. Finally I relaxed and could talk about things other than the one at hand and became again merely someone collaborating to get a job done.

But years passed and the big carrot stayed out of reach. Why did I want partnership? First, if you're gonna work, you might as well go as high as you can. Then, when you're an owner your opinion matters, you have some influence, you're in on the decisions. Almost all your expenses are tax write-offs and your share of the profits is vastly larger than an employee bonus. The partners justified their higher compensation by observing that they shouldered the liabilities—higher risk, higher gain. Right. Never seemed like much risk to me: They carried professional liability insurance for mistakes, and if work dropped off they let people go. Their failure to offer me partnership came down to them not wanting to share. But how much worse off would they have been if they'd invited some eager young people to join them as Ed Haravan had invited them?

I began to realize that partnership wasn't a job classification, nor at this company even a business relationship, but a kind of dysfunctional family membership. They competed over who got which employee assigned to his project. As a favor to Ed they'd hired a young Spaniard for a few months and when he returned to Madrid but didn't work for a fellow they knew, they were distinctly displeased. A "specialist" they hired to develop high-tech business hadn't brought any and he didn't design anything either. Their man in Sacramento hadn't made money and they were fed up with him. They fired a guy the day after he got his license so they wouldn't have to give him a raise. One associate was upset that they wouldn't buy plane tickets for his family to accompany him to a board meeting in Oregon, nor rent a van to take them in, nor even pay for the extra day it took to drive. Another associate left for what he called a job at a real company.

The next year's board meeting was at a crummy Napa resort where they talked about cutting staff back to thirty, which had been their most profitable size. I'd thought for a while that that would be wise since they didn't seem to have whatever it took to run a large company and loved being in absolute charge of everything. I disagreed with their other plans, which anyway didn't go beyond scheming about which markets it might be worth pursuing next quarter. My suggestions were ignored.

I got tired of idiotic political discussions with overeducated farm boys who had assumed their clients' politics, tired of hearing about how we should leave politics to the experts, how technology would solve the world's problems, how we should work hard, meet our deadlines and shut up. I felt like I'd crawl out of my skin.

The work was boring, too. Your first building is exhilarating, the second feels good because you're starting to know what you're doing, you're still learning on your third though much is repetitive, and after that they're all the same. Furthermore,

I didn't want to be broken, didn't want to give up my literary aspirations, didn't want to push the wheel around with my nose in the hindquarters of the horse ahead, didn't want to become dumb, my spirit dulled, so accustomed that I forgot there were other scents than a horse's ass.

It was time for a change. But what? I groaned at the thought of more study and another test but passed the fire protection engineer licensing exam. Okay, now what? Engineers are at the bottom of the design and construction heap. They're blamed for everything that goes wrong, the pressure is terrific, and the liability is high. Small firms have idiosyncratic owners who serve nincompoop developers enriching themselves at the expense of everyone else. Large ones insist on conformity to the corporate ethos, and if you're not promoted you're stuck doing the same thing even more than you would be at a small one; and the large ones don't merely serve capital—they are capital. Most government engineering is defense-related and defense is the distillation of destruction, and the civilian side of government is run by the rich for their own profit as even my dad came to see, though he preferred that to working in the private sector.

A client told me about a project management position at UCSF. During the interview I said that I wanted to work for a place whose bottom line was not profit and that I thought a university, hospital and medical research center were worthwhile endeavors. The boss sounded surprised. "That's unusual, but people do have different motivations." She hired me.

I was excited. There would be more responsibility, more authority, broader involvement in projects, encounters with people from many fields, new things to learn, less intense deadline pressure and liability, better pay. It could lead to overseas or humanitarian work. I wouldn't have to spend such long times on a single subject, and though I might miss battening down on a design problem, and I wondered if dealing with lots of people would drive me crazy, and I wasn't sure I would know when it was my place or someone else's to make a decision, I was eager to try it all.

It so happened that one of my first tasks at UCSF was closing out a project Haravan had designed. Just before the final owner/engineer/contractor meeting I took a look at the rooftop equipment.

Good old Ernie showed up late as usual. "Sorry I'm late. I walked the job before coming in."

Funny I hadn't bumped into him. "Is there anything left to be done?" I asked.

"Nope. They've done a good job."

"Has the dry cooler been painted?"

"Yep. All done."

Funny I hadn't seen the paint.

I don't like liars. He and Haravan didn't get any more work while I was there.

PUBLIC SECTOR II :
PROJECT MANAGEMENT

Good Bosses

My boss Katharine was a very intelligent woman who grasped situations quickly, cheerfully said exactly the right thing to often hostile or demanding people, and let her project managers do their work. She frankly admitted she didn't know what we did. She said, "You do your job, I do the politics." This helped immensely because our clients were difficult. They were doctors. Doctors are trained to assert themselves, to act as if they know all and never err, to be demigods; and many of these doctors were at the top of their academic fields, several were Nobel aspirants, and they'd gotten there through uncompromising ambition and determined infighting. They were our clients because they had huge grants for building and staffing laboratories for their research projects. We did the building. We spent their money and wasted their time. They saw no reason for our involvement—they could easily manage the crude complexities of contract law and ignore the design, bid and build process when it impeded the nobler needs of medical research. Their arrogance and capacity for throwing monkey wrenches was breathtaking. My colleagues joked that it was training for hell.

But my hunch had been right—I enjoyed the work immensely. The projects involved architects, landscape architects, civil, structural, mechanical and electrical engineers, acoustical and lab consultants, the hazardous materials consultant and contractor, the cost consultant, the budget, the funds, the schedule, the project neighbors in the building, the neighborhood residents, the principal investigators and their assistants, the deans, vice chancellors and sometimes even the chancellor, the UC Office of the President and the Regents, contracts, change orders, negotiations, liquidated damages, inspectors, state agencies and their inspectors, the facilities group, parking department, infection control committee, the lunatics in the psychiatric hospital. They all needed to be heard and made to feel they'd been heard. It was fun!

I learned with surprise that frugality was sometimes expensive—it was cheaper, for example, to demolish and install new ductwork than to reuse what was there. I learned when to spend generously and when to bargain. It was strange not having to clock what I did every quarter hour, and some days I left feeling that I'd produced nothing but eventually I realized that my job was to have others produce something. I learned who to go to for information, who to tell what, and who to involve in decisions. Some people insist on deciding, some pass the buck, and some would just as soon have you do it. I learned that if you nudge people along, things happen. I made sure they did their jobs, had the information they needed, and made the decisions they had to make. I did my best to sort out disputes over space and funds and only went to Katharine when issues spread beyond the project.

I was in charge, and it was great having the authority to do what was decent. I could admit mistakes or lack of knowledge, and people forgave me and helped. Of course, it was in their interest since I controlled the money.

A contractor took me aside one day to ask for an extra for his painting sub. "Why?" I asked. "We didn't add any work."

"Well, he really underestimated when he bid. He's done a good job without complaining, and I told him I'd ask you at the end."

Some of my colleagues would have let him be screwed, both him and the contractor who to win the job had probably forced him to honor his bid but agreed to split the loss. I paid; it was a fair price for what the University had received.

I got away early now and then to help at my kids' school. I chaired their building and grounds committee, became a trustee, and was their longest-serving president. I learned a few things about volunteers: They work because they want to, not because they have to—they want to do some good, help somebody, contribute something. Their compensation is satisfaction and appreciation, or companionship, or diversion from boredom; though some demand reverence for their sacrifices or interminable hearings for their closely held opinions. A few arguers and complainers will be damned if they do what they're asked—they're not being paid so they won't take orders. All in all, though, they're the best and most generous of people.

My colleagues at work had rather conventional interests in cars, sports, house prices and stocks, though two gambled seriously on horses. We often met for lunch with a glass or two of wine. I did my hard thinking in the morning those days and made phone calls in the afternoon. But things were changing: When the bar across the street became a coffee shop I noticed that half the bars in town had already been converted. We wore jackets and ties, but the large private companies began letting employees wear jeans and no tie on Fridays for a dollar donation to charity. We took it a step further by foregoing the donation.

A lot of campus people didn't like Katharine's open and sassy style (she was African-American) and forced her out when her own boss retired. We were sorry to see her go. Her operations manager Sandro, a cultured, reasonable and calm man, a great boss, ran the office while they looked for a replacement. I told him once that I thought ten percent of people do all the work. He disagreed—he thought everybody tries to do a good job but they are distracted or inhibited by the system or their own problems.

The replacement came from a Tennessee college where no one expected more than a cheerful manner, agreements were reached over golf, and nobody worried because they knew that in time their own cut of the pie would come. This guy thought he could schmooze his way out of anything. The project managers laughed at him and the clients gave up expecting anything from him. He was so unsuited for the fast-paced urban campus that he was soon moved to the small in-house architectural group.

I sat on the next hiring committee. It was funny how many ill-suited people applied. A project manager from our group completely quashed his chances by acting like the job was his and smiling instead of answering questions during the interview. We chose an administrator from the school of medicine who knew little about construction but got along with everyone. She was a good choice. Henrietta read books on management and took classes on construction law, made a point of walking by once a week to ask if we needed anything, held regular staff meetings, and took care of politics. Henrietta was the third good boss there. They talked to everyone and anyone about everything and anything, and they let us do our job.

Leadership and Command

Our understanding of leadership has been perverted by the business and management appropriation of features of military thinking: mission statements, performance goals, human resources (with its overtones of machine-like interchangeability), strategic campaigns. Leadership is something driven forcefully downwards from the top while those below perform as required.

True leadership is not imposed but communicates moral energy to those who need it. To inspire their followers, leaders must communicate their zeal and an inner faith in themselves and their mission, but the relationship is reciprocal; they must also react and respond. Successful bosses spend more time among their workforce than at their desk, more time listening than talking. Rather than command human resources, they cherish human relationships.

Exclusion

My wife and I weren't getting along and a colleague in an unhappy marriage was charmed by my arty side. The affair lasted one summer and hurt tremendously when she broke it off. It hurt seeing her each day at work. If she saw me at the end of a corridor she turned and took another route. I couldn't go to lunch with the group because she was at the heart of it. In my misery, I wrote. I wrote poems. A friend published two of my stories in anthologies. I wrote a novel and quoted Aeschylus: "...even in our sleep pain that cannot forget falls drop by drop upon the heart, and in our own despair, against our will, comes wisdom to us..." The wisdom that came to me I will share with you: Don't fish off the company pier.

I took up with the facilities group, who were more down to earth than my colleagues anyway. We'd invited some of them to a luncheon once and as we walked back one of the supervisors suddenly turned to me with the joy of solving a puzzle and said, "I know what you are! You're a yuppie!" He meant it kindly but I wasn't proud.

The other project managers followed rules when it was convenient and ignored those that weren't. S and J parked their personal cars in restricted parking stalls. R used the office car for personal business. They flaunted the cell phones we were among the first to have and quickly learned they could respond from anywhere and no one would know they weren't working. Our assistants ostensibly performed routine tasks to free us for more important business, but they trained theirs to do their own work so they could take it easy. They showed up an hour late and left an hour early.

Their loyalty was narrow. They worked on behalf of their clients for the duration of a project but it was clear they didn't care about them, and I sensed an element of malicious delight in working at counterpurposes to the greater good of the institution. They argued with the facilities staff's comments on their design documents instead of acknowledging that these people had to make things work after installation, and they finagled ways to use their services without paying. They gave Henrietta bluster instead of facts, cowed her into believing that she didn't understand project management as well as they did, and condescended to her behind her back. They strutted the millions of dollars they disposed of. They were a clique, a private club, and took satisfaction from excluding outsiders.

I didn't miss my membership but I did feel isolated. I applied to the Foreign Service for an excuse to live apart from my wife without a divorce. My sister had a friend who had an ex-boyfriend at the World Bank, who gave me an introduction to someone in their construction department, who showed interest but said I'd have to take jobs as an independent contractor until they decided to offer me a position. I didn't want to risk an unsteady income while I had young children so it came to nothing. Just as well—I would have been out of place in that neoliberal castle.

Henrietta decided to boost office spirit with a weekend retreat at a bed and breakfast in the mountains. I couldn't imagine being cooped up with the clique and decided to bow out. I also thought the retreat could be criticized as a frivolous misuse of public funds as one at UCLA had been. Though it was none of my business, I shared my thoughts with Henrietta. She said she was sorry that things weren't working for me. Too bad she didn't tell me I was a nitwit.

I liked the work at UCSF and felt that what I served was worthy, and I did some good there. I could have stayed until retirement, but I accepted a job in the Office of the President, which coordinates the systemwide activities of the campuses, thinking the change would broaden my horizon and ameliorate my wretchedness. Henrietta and Sandro both asked if I'd be able to get along with director Michael Nada. He was difficult, they warned, and Henrietta said she wouldn't be able to hire me back if it didn't work out. I figured they were exaggerating; I'd found in grade school that kids get bad reputations merely for being unusual and teachers are called bad when they're simply strict. Me, I found quirkiness interesting and was rather strict myself. Unfortunately, grade school reasoning goes only so far and sometimes I'm too stupid and vain to listen to advice.

Trying To Do the Job

PUBLIC SECTOR III :
BUREAUCRACY

Stuff I was good at, stuff I enjoyed: Managing people and resources, building consensus, dealing with many complex issues at the same time, making decisions, learning new subjects quickly, solving problems in communication and persuasion, negotiation, mediation and dispute resolution, envisioning and implementing improvements, being where the action was.

Stuff I did: Show up at appointments, review documents, write reports, send form letters. I was a paperboy in a marginal side office. Not only did I not write the news, I wasn't even at the scene.

Stuff my boss did: Management by fiat, obfuscation and abuse. Most of the Office of the President operated the same way, by directive and command, no explanations, no involvement in procedural or policy discussions, no questions allowed. This is bureaucracy: The farther you get from real life, from actually producing something, the more obfuscation you meet.

Public sector jobs require navigating among agencies bobbing in an acronymic soup. At the University of California (UC), to receive state funds for its construction needs, each campus prepares project documents (drawings, specifications, budget and schedule) which they submit to the Office of the President (OP or UCOP) for review and forwarding to the State Public Works Board (SPWB) for release of the next phase of funds. UCOP's Capital Development Office (CDO), where I went to work, makes sure that there aren't mistakes in describing the project (such as calling a scholar interaction laboratory a faculty lounge), the State Fire Marshal (SFM) and Division of the State Architect (DSA) have approved the plans, the budget is error-free, and the project schedule matches the state's funding schedule. The CDO is a section of the Budget Office (UCBO), which prepares UC's annual budget.

The state's Department of Finance (DOF), representing the governor, works with all the state agencies to prepare the annual state budget, which is then negotiated with the legislature, represented by Legislative Analyst Office (LAO). After the budget is enacted and signed, the SPWB, consisting of ten people who meet monthly, reviews each project's documents to ensure that its design accords with its description in the budget act before releasing its capital funds. DOF does the review on behalf of the SPWB, so the meetings are a formality unless the LAO has raised concerns. Next, every project expenditure of all agencies except UC and one other must be reviewed by DOF and approved by SPWB according to the process set forth in the immense State Administrative Manual (SAM). You get the picture.

UC has constitutional authority to manage its own finances. Only projects receiving state money are reviewed, and only for release of working drawings and construction phase funds. The funds and expenditures are controlled by its own treasurer, so there is at UC a sense of exceptionalism and a resistance to submitting to procedures that the other agencies follow.

My boss told me, "We don't ask DOF what to do; we tell them what we are going to do." Now, it does save time to give someone the simple choice of approving or not rather than to ask them for suggestions. On the other hand, it can be haughty. As UC's liaison to DOF for state-funded projects, I thought we should work with them, discuss issues, seek and follow their advice. It also happened to be what DOF said they wanted. But Michael Nada didn't trust me alone with them, reviewed my correspondence before it went out, and

before a phone call asked what I was going to say and what
I would say if they then said such and such. If he couldn't go
to a meeting we were to have, he cancelled it.

Bad Bosses

The warnings about Michael Nada were well founded and
his ill nature soon appeared. I suggested that we ask my predecessor Theresa to give me some training before she moved
away. He hesitated for two weeks but finally did invite her to
meet with us. During the two hours that he asked questions
and took notes without letting me say a thing, it became clear
that he didn't know what she'd been doing. In fact, I once
bumped into Theresa's predecessor, who told me that he had
never let Nada know what he did and recommended that I do
the same. Good advice, I'm sure, which Theresa had obviously
taken, but she'd been trained by him and I didn't understand
the system well enough to operate on my own.

At the elevator Theresa offered to talk to me outside the
office, but when I called, her husband wouldn't put her on
the phone because it would upset her too much. I pitied her–
she'd always seemed high-strung. Me, I was calm and got
along with eccentrics.

When I knew Nada better and how thoroughly he was
disliked throughout the system, I emailed her about what
a jerk he was. She wrote back, "I feel that I should have
warned you more about the negative aspects of that position
and I hope you won't hold it against me." (Well, poor thing,
it wasn't her fault I'd taken it.) "I'm beginning to think that
my problem is me, not the jobs I've held. I seem to always
want more responsibility and authority than I have and yet
I get scared to death that I'm not good enough to be doing
what I am doing."

Sensitive people question their ability to perform as well
as they would like. Nada had taken advantage of this to intimidate her into feeling that no matter how well she did, she

could always do better, she wasn't up to snuff, she was worthless. Faced with this you either quit caring or have a breakdown. But I don't readily submit, so I stayed and struggled.

Apart from those two hours, the only training Nada gave me was pithy advice: Be early with things rather than late. Stay ahead of events. Be prepared.

As for relations with the state: Don't force the process. Memorialize exceptions in notes. What is important is the process and developing positive working relationships.

As for the process itself, when it came down to actually doing something: Look in Theresa's files and do what she did.

The CDO was a small part of the Budget Office and enthroned in that heaven was Vice President of the University Michael Ilspach. Presidents came and went—Ilspach bragged of having served seven—but he was the guy who knew where the money was. Money is power and he knew it well.

Heaven was a silent, cold place where gray-haired analysts in suit and tie worked quietly in compartments gathering information from the campuses about enrollment, housing, grant income, and departmental expenses which they reported to Ilspach's political analyst, Eleanor. Once a year he called everyone together to tell them what the legislature was interested in and sent them back to their desks. I thought we should meet more often to talk things over, but evidently there wasn't much to coordinate and nothing to share. Nobody worked with anyone else. Nada actually told me not to waste my time talking to the analysts.

Things ran tranquilly enough—they'd all been there a long time and knew what to do and how to do it—but I foresaw a rocky time when Ilspach finally left, since he alone knew what the moles were doing and where the burrows led. The next person to come was going to find a fragmented culture of silence.

Obfuscation

I had thought information was shared to get a job done. Here, it was brokered. Everyone got a slightly different or partial version of the facts. Nada said so many different things to different people that even I, who as his assistant was presumed to know, often didn't understand what he really meant. He told a campus that if UC submitted working drawings for approval without the SFM or DSA stamp we forfeited any chance to request a budget augmentation. I checked this with DOF, who said it wasn't so, and assuming that he hadn't known, I told him. He replied unpleasantly, "That understanding is with the campuses, not DOF," meaning that I should have known he lied to them and shouldn't have asked DOF.

Sometimes he took me to a campus to explain the state funding process. On the rare occasions that he let me speak, he contradicted what I said and gave his own instructions. Unfortunately, they were often wrong and I would spend the next few days fielding questions and explaining that no, EIRs don't need to be completed before the funding request, and yes, that's right, the P submittal only needs outline specifications.

Bidding needed to be complete before the end of the fiscal year for certain projects, but he gave the impression that contract award must be complete. He did this, he confided to me, so that they would work harder to finish what they did need to do with time to spare.

If the low bid was less than budgeted, the campuses wanted, of course, to keep the difference as contingency funds. Michael told them that "bid savings" were reverted at once, meaning that the difference was returned to the state. This was indeed part of the public contract code but hadn't been enforced in the case of UC. However, DOF had begun asking me to report bid results. Michael refused to believe me, and he was incensed at the thought of them meddling in his affairs, since what he did was "sequester" the money by releasing all funds but the "bid savings" to the campus. If they did run out of money and ask for an augmentation, he would after a suitably disquieting delay give it to them saying he'd pulled strings in Sacramento on their behalf.

He hated questions. Questions were traps. If his interlocutor had more influence than he, a vice-president, say, or someone from DOF or LAO, he feared giving an unwelcome response. If it was a colleague or subordinate, he feared revealing ignorance. He prepared himself for meetings with inexhaustible, precise and irrelevant information, since the more he appeared to know, the more impregnable he was. An interminable recitation of fact after fact in strictly enunciated elegant multisyllabic words either intimidated or numbed his interrogator into dropping the matter.

Trying To Do the Job

Over the years, the DOF staff assigned to UC projects and the UC staff assigned to state-funded projects had reached accommodations to work around several antiquated provisions of the State Administrative Manual. I arrived at CDO the same time a new DOF staffer was assigned to UC. Shawna was young, inexperienced and unimaginative, so she did things by the rules, and the rules were what the SAM said they were. I tried to tell Michael that the old "understandings" he valued so much were gone but he didn't believe me. Shawna told me, for instance, that her boss, Tess, was trying to standardize procedures across all the agencies and UC would have to start using the state's budget format. Michael told me DOF was cracking down because I wasn't performing well.

One day Shawna asked that bid results be reported henceforth as required by the SAM. I told Michael and Eleanor, who said, "Tell her we don't think we should."

Against my better judgment, the next time I talked to Shawna, I did. She gasped and said, "Let me tell Tess what you said."

Ten minutes later Eleanor and Michael called me in. "Tess just called to ask what UC thinks it is doing. What happened?"

"I told Shawna what you told me to say—that we don't think we should report bid results."

They stared at me like I'd shat on the carpet. "Thank you, Jack," said Eleanor. "You can go."

DOF was planning to revise the SAM and asked for comments. Some weeks later Michael mentioned that UC was going to be late with its comments. I told him I'd made some notes; would he like to see them? "Hell no. They can damn well find their own errors."

Eleanor saw me outside the copier room. "I'm meeting with Michael in fifteen minutes to discuss how far we should comply with the SAM. Are you coming?"

He was at the copier so I asked, "Do you want me to join you?"

He turned to Eleanor. "I wanted this to be a high-level discussion."

It didn't matter that I was the one person in all of UC who regularly ensured compliance with the SAM.

Michael and I had sandwiches in Sacramento with Tess and Shawna. (There was no question of alcohol—I never saw anyone at either OP or DOF have a drink.) He prevailed upon Tess to let him pay, and on the ride back told me he had an off-the-books fund for things like this. I asked if I could use it to get to know Shawna better. He wouldn't hear of it. So much for developing positive working relationships.

He told me that Tess had asked him to bring progress sets for all projects being proposed for new funding. I relayed the request to the campuses. Over the next two months they worked hard and their consultants worked hard and I kept Michael informed and he told me how to prepare the material for presentation.

I mentioned to Shawna that we were working on it and she was surprised. "Tess didn't want to see progress sets and estimates. She only wanted a discussion at the site visit level of detail, and only for projects that didn't have site visits. Michael and Tess should talk."

I told this to Michael and he replied, "Then Tess's requirements have evolved. I'll discuss it with her next week when I see her in Sacramento."

"Shawna thought it would be good for you to talk sooner rather than later. She also asked about a budget spreadsheet she gave you."

Twenty minutes later he told me that he'd talked to her. "It looks like we won't have to do the reviews," continuing over his shoulder as he walked away, "that would be good."

"Let me know, so I can tell the campuses what to do." When I asked a couple days later, he frowned and said, "I told you we don't have to prepare the documentation."

He hadn't understood what Tess wanted in the first place. And now it was up to me to placate the campuses for their wasted time, effort and money.

Abuse

Abuse has certain universal characteristics.

My colleague Cathy and I noticed that Nada gave confusing or contradictory information to cover up for not knowing something, or forgetting it, or making a mistake. Being vague also let him deny that he'd meant what you'd thought he said. Sometimes we wondered if he deliberately withheld information from us so he could have the pleasure of being upset when we didn't know something. Humiliating people and making them feel worthless is an obvious form of abuse. Poor Theresa had internalized it and ended up doubting her own abilities.

When he didn't know how to do something he told me to

"find past models in Theresa's files" and "use the same rationale." When I asked questions about the examples I found,
he acted as if Theresa hadn't known what she was doing or
told me that I was misinterpreting it. So I changed names
and dates and sent the models into the blue. One day Tess
called me to complain that we weren't talking to them enough.
I should have told her that Michael had directed me to copy
Theresa's letters and not talk to her, but I didn't.

It didn't take long to learn that you couldn't rely on what
he said but that he was less apt to renege on something he
wrote. So I emailed, "When you interviewed me, I mentioned
that I had planned a week's vacation sometime in late October or November when my son's class goes to Yosemite. I
don't yet know the dates, but it looks like early November."

He wrote back, "Jack — We try to be accommodating with
personal situations such as your son's trip, but request that
people check in advance to make sure that the date is feasible.
It gets touchy in September in particular because the Regents
Budget for Capital Improvements goes to press sometime
between the end of September and the 12th of October, and
everybody in Capital Development contributes (all three of
us!). I am trying to schedule a vacation myself immediately
after we get the Regents Budget to press, and trying to figure
out when that will be."

It was July—this wasn't enough far enough in advance?
Furthermore, he had hired me knowing this. And what did
November have to do with October 12? And what was the
bullshit about scheduling his own vacation? I should reschedule mine to suit his? No matter; he was showing who was boss.

Soon he let me know that email was too informal for
scheduling time off. We (all two of us) were to fill out a request form with name, date submitted, dates requested, and a
line for his large undecipherable signature and small, crabbed
approval date. Sometimes he didn't get around to signing so
Cathy and I took our vacations without approval.

He did not give approval at once, anyway. The request

must be discussed and the discussion was deferred. If the discussion was too late, the request could be denied due to short notice. I once thought to do a favor by submitting in October a request for time in January; he said we would discuss it in January. Advance notice wasn't the point—supplication was the point.

Employees could not accrue more than two years' worth of vacation time so that they benefitted, said the policy manual, from the regular rest they deserved. I had twenty-five days a year by then. Michael told me we were too busy for an occasional day off and that I should forfeit my time as he did. I didn't, though.

Then he began asking for advance notice of sick leave. Cathy and I never figured out how to predict our illnesses, but we did try to schedule doctor appointments on days he would be away.

Abuse operates best in secret. The abuser cannot have witnesses. Like domestic abuse, most workplace abuse takes place behind closed doors. Michael Nada took you into his messy office, closed the door, and berated you for causing his problems. He abused you orally and put nothing in writing.

Salary negotiations happen to take place in secret too, an interesting parallel.

On my first anniversary in June my pay rose three and a half percent. A memo in July to all employees said that funds would be available in October for a two percent merit increase. When my paycheck hadn't changed by November I asked Michael about it. "You need to have been here a year before being considered for a raise," he articulated. He was forgetting or ignoring that I'd been there sixteen months, and it seemed that he didn't know about the raise in June. It was clear that he didn't favor one now. I said no more so as not to jeopardize what I had received.

The next year a form letter from Michael Ilspach announced a one percent merit increase effective November. Some days later Michael told me confidentially that I shouldn't expect a raise. "There is resentment about how much you're being paid. You are one of the highest paid people here and a raise would be difficult."

Well, who had offered me the salary in the first place? He or they had wanted me at it or he or they hadn't, so why try to make me feel bad about it? Who resented it? How did they know anyway, given the secrecy about salaries?

We learn as children not to discuss family income. In the public sector they tell you that revealing salaries can lead to resentment from those making less: Be discreet and keep the workplace calm. The private sector tells you the same but more is at stake: Unlike a public employee who can be told that salaries are fixed by inviolable policy, a private employee can (theoretically) negotiate a raise at any time. Since silence, ignorance and isolation enable lower salaries, the private taboo on talking about them is more severe. In both sectors only people at the top know who makes what.

I asked Michael, "Are you saying I won't get a raise?"

"If you do, it will be only the minimum statutory raise. I got you the highest possible salary when you came because there would be few opportunities for raises afterwards, due to the high salary."

"I hadn't understood that when I came." (That's it, throw his own language at him.)

"Theresa did more work for less money, and she had good political sense." (That's it, suggest I'm deficient.)

Two days later he silently handed me a copy of Ilspach's form letter.

I was drying my hands in the men's room when he came in and began talking. He entered a stall, closed the door, pulled down his pants and took a crap all the while issuing instructions and directions. I was astonished and mildly disgusted but although I could have suggested continuing later and elsewhere, I stayed to see how far he would carry it. He stopped talking only when the flush drowned his voice, and then he resumed.

My computer's power supply failed. He didn't believe me at first and told me to see if I could get along without it. I worked on paper until I couldn't produce a report for Eleanor, who told him to get me a new computer. Then he had someone come to repair the old one.

He had asked me to find a letter and tell him if it made sense. He walked in one day and before he started talking I handed it to him, since I'd learned that to convey anything I had to get it in before his second sentence. He exhorted and preached and left. There was no time for questions, he was irritated by discussion, and he walked away while I was speaking even if I was answering a question he'd just asked. "Here's the letter from General Counsel about CEQA. It makes sense."

He didn't take it. He said what he'd come to say and made as if to leave. I handed him the letter again, and again he didn't take it. He asked, "Does it make sense?"

"Yes, it does," I said.

He talked of something else and again made as if to leave. Again I handed him the letter and again he asked, "Does it make sense?"

"Yes, it does," I said again. This time he took it and left.

I asked if we should submit a certain project package at the cost index for working drawings or construction.

"We never submit working drawings until there is a C appropriation, *do we?*" Sarcastically.

"Well, you've told me that we send working drawings after the first of July at the C cost index so the supplemental language is in place for the higher amount."

"Look in Theresa's files and see what she did."

Vague threats, intimidation, and obfuscation in an email to a campus about a project: "When I visited back a few weeks ago, there was discussion about some of the concerns inherent

in a State project. The plans provided my office have a way
to go. The amount of circulation area, the large ocular with
elaborate shading systems etc in the auditorium... But even
more of concern are various smaller red flag types of items
such as ornamental glass railings, white oak veneer, panel-
ing, and Italian Veneer Plaster in the auditorium, wood strip
flooring, kitchens, bicycle lockers, etc. By the way, shall we
discuss the cost effectiveness of the 'curved steel tubes' of the
high roof framing plan? Four elevators needed? The campus
also of course has to resolve various design conflicts apparent
in the drawings. And, let's see... where is the spill center, and
where is the conference center? Basically we knew this set of
drawings would be produced on an emergency basis given
the start date, but it shows it a little too clearly.

"I have just come back from a meeting on the cost of UC
buildings, and am quite happy to remind people of why we
try to do a good project management job on our own. Others would be quite willing to do it for us if we don't! But if
anyone is unclear on the issue, please let them know that this
project has to pass through the State review process, and doing so at great cost to the project control credibility of the
University is not acceptable."

He didn't give advice or suggestions because he simply
wanted to badger them, make them good and nervous.

The Bitter Young Man

A friend of mine invited me to a Rotary Club lunch. Before
eating, each person stood and gave his name and occupation.
I said, to smiles all around, "Hi, I'm Jack Oakley. I work in
the Budget Office at UC's Office of the President"—the smiles
widened—"as a bureaucrat." The smiles dimmed and the clap-
ping faded. Bad joke, too abrupt, out of context. Should have
built the context: My office won't allow me to use my brains.
We follow rules, and at best we occasionally manipulate one
or two of them. We don't do anything; we only tell others

what to do. We protect our turf. We're backstabbers.

Naw, damn and blast: I should only have made more out of myself than I was, like everyone else.

The End of the Road

Just before the holidays two and a half years after I started, Michael stopped me in the corridor and said that I might be happier in another job. "You haven't developed a sensitivity to issues in Sacramento," he said, "though I have tried to invite you to lunch with Eleanor, Cathy, and even Ilspach, where such things are discussed. I recall that you said you would look for another job if you got an interior office when we move to the new building. Do you still intend to do so?"

He had with overt malice assigned me an office with no daylight and I had threatened to quit out of pique and a half-formed notion that an ultimatum might make him realize that he didn't want to lose me and the depth of frustration his treatment had driven me to, and that he would change for the better. Of course he wasn't reflective enough for this and I had clumsily revealed how fed up I was. But I wasn't quite ready to quit. "No," I said.

"If you do, please give me advance notice so I can make my arrangements."

"Are you saying that you want me to leave?"

"You should consider what you want to do."

The man never gave a straight answer. He was telling me to go without saying that I was being fired.

Ilspach had hired an assistant budget director and then decided he wasn't going to work out. In a short while they'd found him a good campus job, so I asked Michael for his support getting an open position in the facilities department.

"Well," he said, "They can pay more than we can here."

What did that have to do with anything? "It sounds like we agree the fit is bad, but I'm the one who's supposed to find a job. If you want me to leave, I want your help finding one."

"I don't want to ask around for a job for you because people might think there is a problem here."

In the beginning when I realized how bad Nada was, I had wanted to see what I could make of the situation, hoped things would improve, and hoped he would relax as he saw my competence. I didn't want the reputation of moving from job to job too fast. I didn't want to lose my decent vacation and retirement benefits. One day Nada would retire and I could get his job, or at least someone more reasonable would. By now, my marriage had disintegrated and I had moved out, met someone across the country, and begun visiting her. I didn't want the stress of a new job.

I went to see OP's ombudsman to ask about my rights. I felt like telling him that Michael Nada was a servile, fearful, secretive and pompous courtier who had wanted a secretary who could read his mind, a spy who would ingratiate himself with the campuses and report what they wouldn't tell him, a lackey who would issue his directives, and he was running me out because I had failed to fulfill those hopes. Nada was disorganized and resented organized people who got their work done faster. He worked long hours because he was slow and couldn't delegate because he didn't trust anyone. Since he couldn't do everything himself, projects were delayed, campuses complained, and he blamed Cathy and me for not acting sooner. He was confused half the time and fearful all the time.

Instead I told him that Michael had asked me to leave without being specific about my failings, that I'd worked at UC almost twelve years and done a good job at both UCSF and OP, that I feared this might end my UC career, that I believed in higher ed and wanted to stay in the field. I told him about telling DOF what Michael and Eleanor had told me to say and which Michael now gave as an example of political ineptitude, about his treatment of requests for vacation and computer repairs, that he kept his staff to himself, didn't want them working with others, didn't share, didn't help anyone, and about the high turnover of his staff.

The ombudsman was polite but not particularly interested. He told me that I shouldn't feel rushed to leave. I should continue to reassure Michael that I was seeking another job and that because of my investment of time in the University, I wanted one somewhere in the system and it might take some months to find but that I would continue to do my job while I looked. If I felt he was pushing me to leave, I should contact a certain lady in Human Resources to ask her help in persuading him to give me the time I needed to find an acceptable job. He suggested talking to Michael's boss.

I had tried talking to Michael's boss, but Ilspach had cancelled four appointments. On the morning of the fifth I bumped into him at the elevator. "I'll see you at 11:00," I said.

"If I'm here…"

"I want to tell you how upset I am that Michael is firing me and make some suggestions for maintaining the continuity of the office. It won't take long."

"Oh… Well, I may not stay."

When he arrived ten minutes late his assistant asked if he wanted her to place a call for him. He turned to me and said, "This is going to be a while."

"Okay…"

"A long while." He walked off to get some coffee.

"Shall I have her get me, then?" The back of his head nodded.

Half an hour later he received me. The first thing he said was that he didn't want to discuss Michael without him in the room, and he didn't want to discuss personnel matters. He began talking about the Budget Office after his departure.

"That will take staff continuity and good management. The Capital Development Office lacks both," I said. I suggested hiring an office manager to oversee workload distribution and personnel issues, and then I asked for his support and patience while I found another job in the UC system.

"There should be opportunities at the campuses. Is Personnel giving you any help?"

"No. Michael's trying to keep it a secret."

He didn't say anything.

"I don't think Michael has taken any steps to find a replacement for me."

"He probably doesn't have the authority to do it."

That was the end of our talk. And by the way, who better than him would know about Michael's authority?

I understood that I was on my own. So what did I want? A position at OP, UCSF, Berkeley? Work on the new Merced campus? Maybe it was time to find a job outside the system. But what was I equipped to do? What skills could I offer? Dear Sir or Madam: I'm seeking a high-level desk job writing form letters for good pay and benefits in an atmosphere of mindless caretaking. Current position: Paperboy.

Michael didn't talk to me at all for two weeks. Then came a period of collaring me to complain about one thing or another: I hadn't kept myself informed about my work. I hadn't accepted his invitations to lunch. I didn't lay down the law. I didn't take the initiative. I didn't provide leadership to the campuses, and though there seemed to be no point in telling me now, one of my job functions was to advise them on items that could be challenged in Sacramento. He was aggressive and hostile.

It would have been useless to say what I did: Remind the campuses about schedules, revise their quarterly reports, review their tracking sheets, correct their budgets, fix their grammar, rewrite their space and program descriptions to be more bland, clarify the submittal process. And useless to point out that he made me check with him before talking to them and that he got upset when I laid a law down differently than he would have. He was rehearsing the blame he would throw on me afterwards for everything that went wrong.

Time passed. "So how are things going with the job search?" he asked.

"I've had two interviews." I didn't want to be an engineer again, so I'd talked on the phone with a project management firm and a construction company. They'd both been tepid—they said that government jobs take the drive out of people.

"Are they for good jobs?"

"I'm only looking for work I'd like to do." But I still didn't know what that was. Bureaucracy's dissociation from reality, his abuse, and my isolation had worked their magic. I'd never been so lethargic.

"Good luck," he said. "We think your skills are such that you are an excellent project manager, but not so good when political games are involved." The royal or editorial or whatever the hell we.

A couple days later I asked him to decide which progress sets to take to DOF and when.

"Why are you asking me?"

"Because if I'm not here it'll be up to you."

"I'd better start looking for someone so I'm not in trouble when you give me two weeks' notice. I haven't so as not to put pressure on you."

After a moment he went on, "I am under pressure to have you leave, and in two months I will be in the position of giving you two weeks' notice."

"Would you leave if you didn't have a job lined up?"

"If there had been an explicit agreement, yes," taut fat lips giving "explicit" a sharp fricative, labial plosive and precise alveolar. Explicit my ass. There had been no explicit agreement.

"Then you're a different man from me. I have a family to support. Do you really expect me to quit with no income?"

"I can see why you don't want to leave if you don't have a job to go to."

"A friend of mine in employment says it takes six months or more to find a job."

"That implies you'll be here two more months."

"In the meantime I've continued to do my best."

"I appreciate that. You have an important job." I didn't respond to that bit of silliness. "Jack, this job involves three things: politics—"

"Let's talk about it another time. Listen, tomorrow I'll be at a job fair for a couple hours."

The job fair was a sea of tables in an auditorium. The positions were for clerks, salespeople, administrative assistants, caseworkers, entry-level jobs at department stores, small agencies, shipping companies, distributors, a few nonprofits—the kind of job I got when I was young. Same thing at the state employment office. My job, whatever it was to be, would be found by calling people I knew, but I didn't know many people outside UC and engineering.

More time passed. The gentlemen's affair was ending. Nada had politely indicated my flaws and failures, and I'd taken the blows chin up, pip pip, to leave without a murmur. But even a gentleman's patience has limits, and one day he said (again) that in two months he would need to give me two weeks' notice to leave whether I had found a job or not.

When I told Tess that Nada had asked me to leave, she said, "He's a bastard," and as a favor told me to continue sending my budgets in the format I had been using; she would wait until I left to insist on the new one. Well, my successor would be faced with a format without past models—no more "do what Theresa did."

A position at Berkeley I was being considered for was restructured out of existence. I was weary and frazzled. I gave up and called Larry at Haravan.

"You want a job?" he said. "Come on in!"

When Ilspach heard where I was going he told me, "We support private industry."

Private industry supports you, you smug SOB. Or rather, hardworking taxpayers like me.

A couple years later as an engineer with Haravan, I accompanied a group of UCOP big shots to evaluate property in Mexico City. Their peacock heads rose from black suit and tie in soft-spoken cool condescension: "The Lieutenant Governor said to me last week..." "Ah, well on Tuesday the Speaker told me..." Their former fraternity brothers were CEOs, directors, brokers pulling in seven or eight figures while they, though running a six billion dollar enterprise, were making a measly two hundred and flying on public airlines. They took their strokes where they could.

Later yet I met three UC women at a conference. One was an old friend who now ran the architectural group at OP. The second had Michael's job in the reorganized budget office and the third was director of planning at San Diego. My friend introduced me saying that I'd worked for Michael Nada.

"CDO must be a much nicer place to work now with you in charge," I told his replacement. "He was the worst boss I ever had."

After a pause my friend said, "He was a difficult person."

"He was a mean, lying son of a bitch," I said.

After another pause the San Diego lady said, "I liked him. He did me many favors."

Favors that were merely the sudden easing of anxiety he himself had created, I could have replied, but the wind wasn't blowing my direction so I changed the subject.

I am still not sure what Michael and the unnamed others meant by good political sense, but it must be true that I didn't have it. It seemed to me that day-to-day bureaucratic maneuvering meant understanding the people you dealt with, knowing which of your objectives they would accept or refuse, how to couch your requests to suit the circumstances, when to initiate a discussion and when to defer one. I was good at all that. Not only did I never lose anything in Sacramento, I was quick and efficient, my part of the show ran smoothly, and the campuses and DOF were complimentary.

Apart from the thrill of being involved in high-level operations that speaking of political sense gave Michael, I think it fundamentally meant belonging to the group that ran the office. And that he did in fact give me their reason for dismissing me: I declined his lunch invitations. I revealed my disinclination to join the inner circle. You can't refuse the call and expect to be kept around. You have to kiss the ass when it's offered.

The Most Useful Thing I Learned There

The management books say everyone gains when you make your boss look good. Here's my corollary: Don't cover for an asshole. Let him dig his own grave.

PRIVATE SECTOR III :
REWARDS

Haravan hired me back as an associate, which was nice of them though alas the monthly breakfasts were no more. The pay was less than I'd been making and I was back to two-week vacations. Once I mentioned to Ed Haravan that I'd had five weeks at UC, and he just shook his head at the unconscionable profligacy in the public sector. Ties were no longer tucked into shirts; in fact, they were worn only at presentations. Drafting no longer used pencils anyway—it was done on computer. I'd missed the implementation of CAD and never did learn how to use it. Hard liquor at lunch had passed away too. There was an occasional glass of wine, but even the contractors and clients were abstemious.

Not long before I left Haravan for UCSF, one of the electrical engineers had moved to Portland and reported that there was a demand for engineering services. Would they like to send a mechanical engineer to start a branch office with him? They asked me, but I wanted to stay in San Francisco. Their second choice was an eager young guy named Tom Thompson. He'd been very successful: Portland was now headquarters, Tom was president, new partners headed new offices in Irvine, Los Angeles, and Sacramento, and Ed worked part-time as he eased into retirement. Sam was managing principal in San Francisco and there was a new partner Nick. Mr. Liar Ernie was still there and he still disliked me.

There was also a new associate principal step on the stair to partnership: You bought nonvoting shares in the corporation which you could sell back at a twenty percent discount if you left after five years, your insurance premiums were paid and deductibles covered, your bonus was larger, and there were twice-monthly conference calls with Tom and the other associate principals wherein he monologued and you were privileged with being given tasks he cooked up. After two years they made me one and gave me shares in lieu of overtime pay.

Once a year they decided how many new shares to offer. They treated it quite seriously, but it all seemed rather puerile to me. I'm afraid one of my career-inhibiting traits was not giving the symbols of business the same weight that others did. Tom and Sam encouraged us associate principals to buy and a couple times gave bonuses to match purchases, but I never spent more than what I was saving on insurance so that if I left I could tell myself I hadn't actually lost cash out of pocket.

Tom operated in two modes: command and pitch. He hadn't a hint of self-doubt and he moved too fast to notice any mistakes he made. Larry told me the partners joked about his short attention span and his brash, driving style but said he was shaking things up and making them try new things. Not all of them liked it, but they went along. Sam told me Tom once asked if they were ready to jump out of the helicopter after him. War was chic—we'd invaded Iraq, camo was the color, Jeep had a new wave of jingo names: Liberator, Gladiator, Freedom, Liberty, Patriot. The partners said yes sir. It was easier than thinking, the company was growing, and they were making good money.

He brought in speakers to inspire us, passed out questionnaires to help us classify our personalities, and for Christmas gave us books on how to grow our good company into a great one. Sam confided that Tom had a few characteristics the books classed as negative. On visits to the office he chatted with each person, praising and exhorting and issuing directives which he soon forgot. Afterwards we'd sort things out with somewhat amused chagrin. One guy told me that Tom was a dead ringer for his bipolar father.

Tom asked me one Friday afternoon to write a white paper

on solar energy costs and rebates that he could use Monday to impress a client, and assured me that I could call on all the resources of the company. It didn't occur to him that though everyone may have been at his disposal, I would still have to explain to anyone I called on, as well as their boss, why they needed to work over the weekend. "If we get this job," he said, "it will make your career!"

Silly me, I'd thought my career was already made. I worked hard, did a good job, had my clients' respect, brought in projects and developed new markets, made a profit, and expected an offer of partnership. Sam had cautioned me more than once, "It's like a club. The other members have to invite you to join." That was the truth. Not only ownership and promotion but continued employment depended on how much they liked you. They got rid of excellent people merely for being quirky. In six years, seven good engineers out of the forty were fired. You could see it coming when they started grumbling about one odd bird or another. I did my best to seem like I was one of them but I couldn't be authoritarian with employees and wasn't all that interested in how much money we made and didn't play golf.

Assuming that versatility is a virtue and valuable to a business, I once made the mistake of telling Nick that I had a life outside the office. "I can see that," he said, and didn't say it approvingly. They mistrusted versatility and suspected signs of intelligence. Me, I'd thought that if I did my work well and brought a diverse breadth of outlook to the company I would be valued and compensated, but I began to realize that the only way to succeed was to keep my mouth shut. This caused a chronic tension between wanting to say what I was thinking and knowing I should suppress it. I'm sure psychotherapy can help a person resolve this sort of thing, but it can't mitigate the oppression that causes it.

I decried the invasion of Iraq to an up-and-coming associate principal. "Iraq had nothing to do with 9/11. They're no threat to us. Maybe Saddam's a dictator, but we've done business with other dictators, and just two years ago he was our buddy. What's changed? All we're doing is generate ill will in the Middle East and around the world. And if we do want to replace him, why are we attacking the whole country?"

"Because we can."

How do you answer logic like that?

I visited Jordan as the guest of an equipment manufacturer and afterwards vacationed in Turkey and saw solar hot water heaters on the roofs everywhere. On my return I was telling the principals and APs about it as an example of people around the world embracing green technology. The up-and-comer made a face.

"What is it?" I asked. "Don't you think we could do that here?"

"Oh," he said, "they only do it because they don't have an infrastructure."

Sam must have expressed doubts about my commitment and suitability to Tom, for one day Tom took me to breakfast. Chit chat and then, "Jack, sometimes I think you're fighting the French revolution." Meaning, maybe, that I was too free, equal and brotherly with the employees, or that I made too many suggestions for improving things. I reassured him with a catch in my voice, "Tom, Haravan is my life!" That was enough. "That's great!" he said. Just a little breakfast theater.

Tom didn't know the French from the Copernican Revolution, but he was onto something. I was raised to believe in freedom of expression and the obligation to exercise it, and if what I expressed could be called rebellion, it was against the modern descendants of the bourgeois victors who had become the new aristocracy of obscene wealth and power. Nothing wrong with the revolutionary values of freedom to act without imperial constraint, equality before the law, and mutual assistance and cooperation, as I'm sure Tom would have agreed. But what I held as social goals were for him symbols, nodes of nebulous sentiment. That's what happens when everything is packaged for sale.

The social fabric is woven here and comes apart there. Although men are self-interested, we have found that we are stronger together than apart, and out of this discovery was woven the great multipatterned tapestry we inhabit. Theft betrays the trust that keeps it together. Where theft is punished society is just, and where a few possess much and many little, much has been stolen. These days much theft and corruption goes unpunished. Trust evaporates. Each man is of necessity for himself. Things fall apart.

The fabric must be restored. White-collar workers of the world, unite! Together you can force these SOBs to share their profits with you who worked to earn them. You have nothing to lose... but your job. Right. Okay, so don't overthrow the system, don't call a general strike, don't even grumble—just every now and then get together and make a few requests. Fear not, the police and the militia are for unskilled labor, not you, and if five or six people in a professional firm of forty insist on a change or two, they won't be fired. Talk to each other, speak your mind. Do it in their own calm and measured language.

But people are afraid to talk. They're afraid to look each other in the eye. I smile at children on the sidewalk and they look away—I'm the stranger they're not supposed to talk to. I say hello to a fellow at the restroom door and he ignores me. Why, does he think I'll grab his penis? Where has civility gone? Come on, people, if you won't badger your politicians for better schools or decent healthcare at least pass the time of day with each other! Eat lunch together instead of alone at your desk! Think, talk, be friendly!

This was my revolution.

Tom had grand ideas. He wanted to grow Haravan into the largest engineering company in the world. Since they had set up an answering service in Singapore during a project for an American client and hoped for more Asian work, he convinced the partners to rename the company Haravan International. It embarrassed me to trot that moniker out, especially with locals who knew Haravan from way back. Over the years his aspirations dropped to America, then to the Pacific states, and finally International was dropped, which left them with a lot of unusable stationery but was a relief to me.

He set the tone for the company and the tone was sales. Now, I'm not fond of sales myself, but selling is necessary. Customers need to be aware that you're offering what they need. I do draw the line at trying to convince them that they need something which they don't, or that what you have is what they need when you know it isn't. Someone has to sell work to keep the company in business, but under Tom the company was forgetting that the work then had to be done. When Larry retired there was less attention to performance, and my insistence on good and thorough work began setting me apart.

On a flight to Seattle Tom met an advertising guy. Like called to like. Without consulting his partners he hired the adman to jazz up Haravan's image, brand the company, and develop a website. The adman came up with a business card that looked like a coffee cup sleeve with contact information on the front, company promotion on the back and clever sayings inside, all in green to correspond with our new image as a leader in sustainable design. Tom would push the ends together to open the center, while attentively watching the face of the person he gave it to, smiling indulgently at their astonishment. The damn cards were as thick as three ordinary ones; you could carry only two in your wallet. I quietly sliced off the edges and removed the back panel so I could hand out normal ones.

Now that we were leaders in sustainable design, Tom insisted that the principals and APs become LEED accredited professionals. The Leadership in Energy and Environmental Design program recently cooked up by the US Green Building Council to rate the greenness of buildings was catching on with owners and institutions and he felt we should be leaders in sustainability marketing. I'd thought I was finished with certifications, so I groaned and crammed for the exam. LEED has become quite an industry now with rating systems for nine development types, four classification levels, and specialty accreditation. Luckily for me, I was accredited early enough that I'm grandfathered out of the new continuing education requirement.

I suppose this institutionalization of sustainable design is a sign of the laudable trend toward energy-efficient buildings which lessen our impact on nature, but it's irksome to know that you're proficient in something yet must still pay a fee to suffer an exam and another fee for the certificate and more fees for classes afterwards to prove you've kept up with the field and yet another fee to renew the certificate. But if you don't and other things are equal, a client will choose the certified candidate. Luckily for me, too, I began energy modeling, project management, and building commissioning before there were certification programs. In fact, I began working at just about the time people became less willing to give an eager but inexperienced youngster a chance.

During one of the AP calls I was assigned the honor of managing the website development. Tom later told me that I was the only one he trusted to do a good job because I was the most open to things outside of engineering. I couldn't tell if that was the truth or flattery. The adman's team made a kickoff presentation that left me with a poor impression, and as time passed they never met deadlines, requested additional fee for their own delays and ignored my suggestions. Their comparison of hosting services and software was incomplete, and they steered the selection to a hosting service they owned and to software that I discovered they were developing themselves.

I kept Sam and Nick abreast of this and received noncommittal looks and mumbled replies. Finally, wanting to absolve myself when the costs became apparent, I outlined my concerns in an email to the principals under the guise of asking for suggestions about dealing with the problems and unnecessary expenses. There was no response other than Nick telling me the timing was bad and Sam saying that it wasn't worth saying some things. The website was finally launched to great acclaim.

Soon the adman moved from advertising strategies to advising Tom on operations. For example, one of the Sacramento principals just had to go—his clunky, technical style was putting off potential clients. I was so annoyed that I casually mentioned it to the fellow. He didn't like it, but I saw that it was going to take more than a disgruntled principal and AP to get rid of the adman.

Showmanship had taken over. Max, the SF marketing guy, gave up and left.

Tom sent an AP from Portland to help me interview for a project. While we rehearsed, Chuck proposed saying something smarmy and false which I argued against. He was stubborn, but finally agreed not to say it. However, come the interview, he went ahead and did. We got the job and of course it was Chuck's coup, though the client told me later that it was only because of another consultant I'd brought along.

I'd had fun designing data centers and travelling around the country and England and Germany to commission them. I'd helped a UC campus develop its sustainability plan, and for the most part I'd run my own projects. But people like Chuck were succeeding, and though Sam had always treated me like a future owner, he always put me off when I asked when. Another partners' retreat passed. Maybe I should have forced them to choose between having me as I was or not having me at all, but I told Nick that it was clear they weren't going to offer me partnership and I was okay with dropping it if they adjusted my compensation. I got a decent raise, and he and Sam stopped sharing confidences with me.

Max the marketing guy and I had stayed in touch, and one day in a fit of frustration I told him I was thinking about leaving. He talked up his new company, the San Francisco office of a San Jose-based firm, and the next day introduced me to his boss, Norman Manchester. I was hired as a principal to start a new commissioning department.

Sam was very hurt. I guess he thought people weren't supposed to leave unless they were told to. I guess all the partners did. None of them, even the ones I'd been on good terms with, responded to my farewell notes. Ed Haravan, at least, did look sad when I told him I was going to be a principal at last.

The deal about share resale was that you got only fifty percent back if you left before five years. I'd been associate principal for four and a half, so I waited six months and then wrote to ask for my eighty percent. Sam promptly called. "Jack, the clock stopped when you left. It wasn't five years."

"I suppose you could look at it like that, but I own them now and it's been five years since my first purchase. I'm sorry I left so abruptly, but you can see that I hadn't been planning it since I bought some just three months earlier."

"Well, I can't help your timing. It wasn't five years. And we don't even have to give you any money now—we can spread payments over the next five years."

"Wouldn't it be better to get it over with and not have to deal with me for so long?"

"I'll think about it. Listen, Jack, I'm very upset that you've been trying to recruit my staff. That is not honorable. It is not acceptable."

"Come on, Sam, Tom does it all the time."

"He does not!"

I held my peace.

A couple weeks later he asked me to come in. They were only going to give me fifty percent but the office would give me a small bonus to help make up my loss. He scrawled some calculations to show that I would be close to being made whole. And he had the decency to admit that I was right about Tom.

When the check came it was less than he'd said.

(They really were stingy sons of bitches. As someone approached his tenth anniversary with the company they would ask me to find out what he would like as a service award. It could cost up to a thousand dollars but had to be something that looked like a deductible business expense. In my own case, four years after I rejoined them I mentioned that I was proud to have been with them for ten, having been there six the first time. They didn't take the hint. Maybe they figured associate principals didn't need additional rewards.)

Soon afterwards I heard that everyone had been given a raise and four associate principals in various offices had become principals, including my smarmy pal Chuck. Chuck eventually replaced Sam as managing principal in San Francisco, and he was so disliked by the staff that he was quickly promoted to corporate marketing director.

After that I quit standing up for better treatment at work. As in any revolution, the revolutionary himself never benefits.

The Work Ethic

Stephen Dedalus would not serve that in which he no longer believed; I found in what I served that in which I could believe. Any endeavor toward a good goal is worthy of support. My earnestness and diligence took me far, and my bosses appreciated the honest day's work I gave for a day's pay. But those who run the show mistrust anything less than total fealty and their misgivings about my faith created the barrier beyond which I was not invited to go.

I concealed my incomplete commitment as well as I could, but it was revealed in understanding other points of view: that of a contractor with whom I was bargaining, or a competitor's, or a client's when negotiating my company's fee for services. I believe that an enterprise can be run decently and honestly and still do quite well. If asked point blank, the owners and directors I've known would not disagree, but when it comes down to a particular situation, they identify themselves so closely with their organization that accepting less than the most they could gain amounts to personal failure.

Lack of total fealty amounts to ethical failure, too. The work ethic, an integral part of modern Puritan America, carries an aroma of sanctity whose source is lost in antiquity but which misleads the devotee into feeling that by practicing it he fulfills his moral obligations. It also happens to stimulate loyalty in workers, render them more submissive, and inspire contentment and gratitude.

The ethic conceives nothing of the individual's responsibility to the public. Businessmen are too deeply immersed in private affairs to take personal part in the administration of government, yet in the more or less popular form of government that we have the problem of control is not easily solved. The electorate is systematically deluded through the media, meaningless labels and enthusiasms are created, solemn warnings are issued, and national, religious and racial animosities are fomented.

Work is necessary—we are not, after all, lions satisfied with lazing around. We are thinkers and actors and communal creatures. Disciplined minds and bodies are a pleasurable and indispensable component of happiness. Sewage treatment, power distribution, food, and healthcare require the work of many, as do symphonies, bicycles and ping pong balls.

The nineteenth-century transcendentalists formed communities wherein each shared equally its labor and its leisure. This small step up in the status of leisure—the Puritans had equated it with idleness and idleness with sin—has barely held. Leisure today is perceived in the context of work: It is the name given to weekends, holidays, vacations, evenings—any time not spent in the workplace.

Consequently all of life is work.

Is it really?

What if we valued life above work?

Can we purge the work ethic of its religious elements so that a secular ethic of accomplishment and self-development remains? What about an ethic in which employment for pay is valued no more highly than other types of work? I am an engineer who writes and a writer who designs buildings and a father and publisher and student of the piano and martial arts. A job is a means of self-expression only for the few who are so spiritually impoverished that consumption and production bound their aspirations.

Well, a nice idea perhaps, but ethics change when people change—not in response to a better idea. We may as well accept the slow shuffle of change.

PRIVATE SECTOR IV :
A BUSINESS MODEL

The word on the street was that Beta Universal Engineering Company wasn't a good place to work, but I hadn't asked around because I liked Max and I forgot marketing guys are enthusiastic about everything and I was keen to leave Haravan and I'd finally be a principal and build a new department. It turned out principals were cheap—in the twenty-person SF office there were five others.

The founder, CEO, and principal partner was Abdi Abedin, a wheeler and dealer and another great salesman like Tom Thompson though his tactics differed somewhat. He got clients two ways: He bought them with huge parties, private parties, wine tastings, use of his Las Vegas condominium, helicopter transportation, and flights to Hawaii to see projects; and he bought smaller firms whose partners wanted to cash in after building up their practice and backlog of clients.

Two of San Francisco's principals were from a recent merger that included a two-year contract for them and jobs for the employees. The staff began to leave when they found out where they stood at BUEC—designers and drafters were expendable labor. There was no training, good work wasn't valued; what mattered was how little time they spent on a job. The new principals scrambled for help from closely guarded fiefdoms in the San Jose office. The quality of service dropped as good people quit, errors and omissions and change orders grew, and clients left. Soon it was time to buy a new firm.

Abedin wasn't interested in engineering or in managing the company. His leadership consisted of a bi-weekly telephone conference on the profit, loss, and billing status of current jobs. Naturally, the principals had developed some bookkeeping footwork to postpone revealing how far in the red their projects were. It looked like most were. I never did figure out how they stayed in business; it must have been early billing on new jobs that kept them going. Abedin didn't like seeing overhead time because it couldn't be billed. I was on the spot in the beginning because I'd naively assumed that we should track our time honestly so we could see how we spent it, what staff were doing and to whom we should assign work. When questions about resource or staff allocation came up, he told us he was confident we could work it out among ourselves.

SF's managing principal Norman Manchester had merged his company to start the local BUEC office. He told me one day over coffee that he was looking for someone to replace him. I must say I didn't see why he would give up the cushy deal he had. Half the time he golfed and lunched with clients. Now and then he gave his opinion about a design issue, but his usual involvement was dropping in on an occasional client meeting to wow them with our innovative approach to whatever was being discussed. He wasn't interested in office management or production, getting the job out the door, quality control—he left that to the five of us—until he disagreed with something he'd noticed and issued an order ex cathedra.

He did insist that we scrutinize the staff's weekly timesheets to make sure they weren't covering up not being busy. On the other hand, like the San Jose principals who knew the game, he charged all his own time to projects. Mine were regularly hit, which left less fee for staff to actually do the work. Even his wife Carla, who worked part-time as receptionist (her sister worked the days she was off), charged a day to one of my projects. I asked if he knew why. He pursed his lips and said that she had straightened out his files. And in December when he joined us to discuss bonuses, he said with pursed lips and a wink at me, "As I told Jack, Carla does a lot of work on projects," and wrote down a large figure for her. Nepotism is good work when you can get it.

For two months I developed commissioning standards

and procedures and a marketing plan. None of the principals in either office took the time to look at them or answer my calls to talk about how to sell it. Norman was busy selling his own work and Abedin was selling work for San Jose. I called former clients but didn't land anything. Then Norman asked me to resolve some design problems that were showing up on a project in construction. Problems indeed. Several projects had problems. At one jobsite everyone laughed when I walked in—I was the seventh BUEC engineer to be in charge. As I dug into that one, it was clear that no one had ever checked the design.

After that, Norman asked me to help design a new project, and soon there was no time for the commissioning program. Instead, I designed, administered construction, tried to figure out the bookkeeping scheme, worried with the other five about how to deepen the drafting pool and lure good engineers from other companies, hired graduates and fired them when their sense of entitlement and disinclination to learn became clear. I did hire one great young engineer who'd left Haravan, thus performing a service for BUEC and a disservice to him.

One day a San Jose partner called and asked, "You were hired to bring in commissioning work. Where is it?"

There's support and encouragement for you! "I haven't had time," I told him. "I've been fixing all the fucked up projects around here instead."

Abedin bought a construction management firm acting as general contractor on a project and told them to use me as commissioning agent. They didn't want me, which their subcontractors sensed and so wouldn't cooperate with me, and then they were displeased that I didn't bully the subs in return. They complained that I was spending too much time on San Francisco work. I pointed out that I was a principal and had other company responsibilities, and they told me to not bother coming back. Norman said not to worry about it and Abedin never said anything. Things happened without explanation.

I sold no commissioning and only a little engineering. I couldn't. I wouldn't give bribes and had nothing to offer but myself. Though former clients may have liked me, they didn't trust BUEC and knew they'd get better service elsewhere. If I stayed much longer my own reputation was going to suffer. I applied for city jobs but it was like throwing rocks into a dark tank, a plonk when receipt of the application was acknowledged and then silence. I almost took a job at the Golden Gate Bridge as a purchasing agent but the boss was a prune, the pay was low, and the desk was in a windowless portable in the wind and fog.

Then Max announced that the Northern California Community College District was looking for a project manager and if we could find them one they'd owe us a favor. He mentioned a project manager working there named Conrad whom I'd known briefly at UCSF. I called at once.

Conrad set up a meeting with his two co-executive directors. Twenty minutes into the interview Margo rose and said, "You dress well and you don't stink." To her co-boss Steve she said, "He looks okay to me."

Steve gave me the choice of employment with the District or an independent contract but urged the latter; their department had been formed to oversee a bond-funded construction program that would end in three or four years when the money was spent, and it would be easier to let contractors go than find new jobs for employees. It was an easy choice. Self-employment fit well with the publishing business my wife and I had started. I would do project management or engineering as a day job, and edit and publish until it brought in enough to cut back on eight-to-five work.

As I returned my computer to BUEC's IT techie, who happened to be Abedin's nephew, he surprised me by saying, "I thought you were supposed to take over the SF office."

"Hah!" I laughed. "They should have told me." Not that it would have made any difference. Who wants to run a small fiefdom under constant attack?

I was glad to be going back to higher education, where among other things there are institutional checks on fraud. Workplace behavior in the private sector is ultimately based on money. If you're making a profit for the company you can get away with abuse, mistreatment and murder. And you're more highly compensated, which in itself earns respect and better treatment.

In the private sector, work trumps everything. Take Gordon Getty, one of the richest people in the world, who happens to have a passion for opera. Not only does he donate generously, he writes it. During the production of his first opera he was interviewed about his creative habits. Now, you would suppose that he has the wherewithal to take time off whenever he likes, but he said that if the phone rings while he is composing and a business affair wants his presence, he puts the music aside. May he be our model, Mr. Getty.

You have to eat lunch—do it with a client. Go to their office parties. Public service is good marketing. Contribute to the boss's charity and solicit donations for your own. Ride a bike for epileptic children or mentor a kid in a high school science class. Join a professional society, give a speech, publish an article, teach a class at the junior college, build sand castles on the beach with people from your industry. All this is considered when promotion time rolls around.

Hobbies are great things, and families too. The announcement they send around when you're hired includes a few personal nuggets: He likes to camp, she's a cake decorator, he coaches his daughter's soccer team. This shows your human side. But don't talk about your spare time too much, maybe a little chitchat on Monday morning or after a holiday. Do not tell anyone that you write fiction. It may be acceptable if you're on the verge of riches and fame; otherwise it runs up against the American anti-intellectual streak.

Don't talk about yourself, in other words. Talk about sports—not the golf you played but the game you saw on TV—football, baseball, basketball. If you want a reputation for unconventionality, talk about hockey. Choose topics from the shared experience, the communal life, the presidential debate, what you saw on last evening's news. You'll find you don't need a TV to keep up with the news. When you've heard two people use the term fiscal cliff or weapons of mass destruction or the North Korean threat to world peace or how pensions are busting the budget, you know what was covered last night and which opinions your town or state or country leaders want you to have about what they're planning to do next.

This goes for the public sector as well, though things are a bit more relaxed and you're not always selling.

I was looking forward to that, and I was glad to be getting out of the myopic engineering world and to being a project manager again, where among other things people would laugh at my jokes.

PUBLIC SECTOR IV:
WORK DESPITE THE BOSS

This was the second bond-funded construction program at the Northern California Community College District. The first had been run by the project management firm TND which reported to the vice chancellor for facilities, Ignacio Ortega, an affable ex-military fellow who provided executive leadership and left day-to-day operations to TND. Margo Tuchman was facilities director at the time and felt that TND hadn't included users in decision-making and, worse, failed to properly document and close out the projects. She and the director of purchasing, Steve Campbell, were in an MBA program with NCCCD's chancellor, and the three of them wrote a business plan for a capital project management department. The chancellor then proposed one with her and Steve as co-executive directors to the board of trustees, catching Ignacio completely by surprise. The chancellor did heed Ignacio's advice to not fully dispense with TND's services and keep them on to manage construction. Management of design, furniture, commissioning, and move-in was assigned to the Construction Planning and Management (CPM) department.

Conrad liked it much more than the job he'd left at UCSF. It seemed the project managers there had succeeded in shifting all their work to outside project management firms and only showed up for meetings where they could act important. "And the whole place is so procedure-bound you can't get anything done. Not like here, where things are still being formed. It's a lean and mean organization."

The Mean

It was a fact universally acknowledged that Margo was an asshole. Anger was her mode and dissatisfaction its expression. She was the only person who knew how construction projects should be managed. She insisted on making all decisions and if she wasn't involved in one woe betide the staffer who had excluded her. She was quick to point out failure. She offended everyone. Her staff feared her, contractors and consultants rolled their eyes, and District administrators and faculty didn't understand why it took so long to get things done.

She was scared and didn't want anyone to know how scared she was. She was afraid of making a mistake, afraid her department would fail, afraid to trust her staff. When she'd been maintenance and operations director she could boss around the laborers, custodians, mechanics and electricians, but now she was directing educated professionals, several of them more experienced than she. She'd consoled herself by hiring a few people with no construction experience from whom she picked a couple to mentor, which didn't stop her from insulting them about their ignorance or complaining about it to others.

She got mad when
    you didn't do what she said to do (because the work was unnecessary or counterproductive).
    you did what she said to not do (because her command was dead wrong).
    you did what you thought she said to do (you'd misunderstood or she'd omitted key information).
    you didn't do what she didn't say to do (she'd forgotten to tell you).
    you did what she said to do (she'd forgotten she'd told you, or she'd changed her mind and hadn't told you).

The Lean

Despite being co-executive director, Steve was as brow-beaten as everyone else. She ignored him, and soon others did too—people would even start talking before he had finished. But he was also the boss, he was the cost guy—she wasn't interested in costs—and you couldn't ignore him entirely. He did have good sense about how to present things, about what would and wouldn't fly with whom. He was a decent fellow and tried hard but was far too picky—a good quality in purchasing agents, but construction projects need a more relaxed approach. Sometimes you don't have time, in order to keep things moving, for a deal based on more than imprecise information.

The District used the design-build method of contracting and had selected Gerston-Oliver Construction Company for the projects at Hilltop College that I managed. Now, a supposed benefit of design-build is that the contractor does whatever is necessary to build the project for the contract price, assuming the owner doesn't add scope or make late changes. GOCC performed the way they were supposed to and sometimes even threw in things for free, like a railing the facilities group asked for long after the design was complete and the subcontracts were let. I told Steve so he'd know how decent they were being, but he was displeased that the work hadn't been documented as a no-cost change order. I told him I wasn't going to ask them to spend more time and effort on free work, and after a while I stopped mentioning these things.

The contract included $600,000 for steel price escalation. After a year GOCC told us they hadn't needed to use it all and offered to return the remainder by doing some change order work at no cost. Steve insisted on figuring out how much the work was worth to find out if they were being fair. I pointed out that the money was theirs, it was not an allowance, the District had given it to them in the contract, and they were doing a favor by giving us anything at all. No, no, no—Steve convened four of us to estimate the costs ourselves, and when they seemed to be less than earlier GOCC estimates he was of the mind that we shouldn't do a change order accepting the free work until he hashed things out with them.

GOCC's project manager rolled her eyes when I told her. "We don't have to give you anything, you know."

"I do know," I said. "Be patient."

Steve kept pushing for a meeting and I kept putting him off until I was able to get Ignacio's ear. Ignacio talked to Steve and that was finally that.

There was a contract allowance for installing security cameras around the campus. After a good deal of effort designing, reviewing and redesigning, questioning cost breakdowns and examining revised subcontractor quotes, the time came when the work had to start. To get GOCC going I negotiated a simple, flat reduction in cost and ran it by Steve. He grumbled that we didn't have a breakdown of the reduction and the price was high but told me to write the change order, which he approved, Ignacio approved, the VP of Finance approved, and it was executed. Then he told me he still thought the trenching costs were too high and wanted to meet with GOCC and the sub.

"The trenching's already been done," I said.

"Good, we can compare the actual cost to the estimate."

"But we already agreed on the cost."

"But if the cost is wrong it should be changed."

"If you ask for actual costs now, doing the paperwork will drive everyone crazy and we'll get a breakdown showing they equaled the proposal or more. Besides, they'd see this as reneging on our deal. We need to keep their goodwill and trust, Steve."

"I have to leave for a meeting," he said. "Let's talk about this again."

But he didn't bring it up again, thank goodness, and neither did I.

Staff Relations

The District was building five hundred million dollars worth of assorted projects simultaneously. Margo demanded that we do everything—make sure the users, the college cabinets, and the maintenance and operations staffs were included in design decisions, review all the contractor submittals, check the costs of change orders, take photos for the website and update the descriptions of project status, prepare presentation materials, count parking spaces, coordinate bus stop relocations with the bus company, keep the campus maps current, help organize ground-breaking and dedication ceremonies, ask the contractors to buy lunch for the ceremonies—and Steve would want different things at the same time.

When faced with so much to do, you have to concentrate on the important things. Now, I can set my own priorities, but when I was given too many contradictory instructions and demands, I figured that rather than complain about not having enough time to do everything they asked, I'd make them sort out their own priorities by asking them to help set mine. They never answered. I'm sure they had more important things to do.

Margo started staff meetings with a stab at endearing herself. For example, when someone remarked about my fountain pen she commented, "Jack's fancy schmancy pen."

The agenda listed topics for her and Steve and occasionally someone else to present, but she couldn't bear two minutes passing without taking over. She loved telling us how to do things—she probably should have been a teacher—and not only did not ask for suggestions but ignored us if we insisted on making one. She was a smart cookie but was nonplussed when presented with something she didn't know. She stared at you with stony blankness and after a moment's silence resumed the lecture, but now it was about her need to be told things in a timely manner.

Nothing satisfied her. She had her own problems, of course. Her mother never thought her daughters were good enough and she was uncomfortable with people outside the context of work. She was so determined to appear to be in charge that she wouldn't laugh at a joke—it was a chink in her invulnerability.

My assistant Leonora and I were thankful not to be with her in the West Bay College mother ship. Our colleagues there told us how lucky we were. They eventually got so upset that Margo's boss heard about it and sent her to a management class. For a couple weeks we all received emails thanking us for our good work. Then there was an office lunch where she sat silently until the end when she said a few words about how well we are all doing. Even months later she occasionally sent a stiffly worded thank you note.

It was hard to take those thanks seriously since they were coming from chapter eight of some management manual, but it was better than being berated. And there was some comfort in knowing that civilization, embodied in upper management's concern, mild though it was, had extended its tempering fingers into our office.

Was she capable of change? we wondered. Would acting appreciatively engender true appreciation? Does one become courteous by following courtesy's forms?

GOCC's project manager and I were talking about her one day. "We think she's almost a good manager," Ursula said.

"Do you think she can become one?"

"Nah. She won't change."

I had to agree; but one can hope.

Abuse

At UCOP, Michael Nada's abuse tended toward the domestic variety, in private and behind closed doors. Margo's was more often in full public view, and she bullied the weakest and most defenseless.

When I started, the CPM offices were in a building at West Bay College that was to be demolished. Fortunately for me and Leonora, the new offices were too small for us so we were sent to a building at Hilltop College that would be demolished but could house us in the meantime. The Hilltop landscape maintenance group was storing rakes and lawnmowers there until their own building was finished, and the facilities director cajoled me into letting the equipment stay in the part we wouldn't be using.

Margo said the equipment had to go. She talked to Ignacio, the facilities director's boss, and Ignacio agreed with her.

Three months later when we had to move again, Margo said to Leonora, "Be sure you don't agree to sharing your space with the lawnmowers again."

Margo knew very well that it was I who had agreed. Why was she going after Leonora? Was she disinclined to insult me directly and using Leonora as a proxy? Was I being offered membership in the fellowship of bosses who let their staff take the fall? Or was it simply because Leonora was weak?

I had to defend Leonora. "I was the one who agreed to that," I said with a smile and a laugh to soften my contradicting her.

Margo stared at me. After a moment Steve said, "We should move them in here for your last two weeks so you can see what you were missing." I laughed again to pretend it was all a joke.

Margo often told Leonora that she shouldn't have let me do one thing or another, and then Leonora thought she was failing. I told her to ignore it because what Margo said wasn't fair—nobody can expect someone to stop her boss from doing something he's determined to do.

You couldn't catch Margo in the hall for a question. That was stepping on other people's time.

"Margo, would you like me to arrange the meeting about the loop road to include Serge, Ignacio, Wanda and Christine as well as you and Steve and GOCC and Don Bridges? That way if GOCC comes back beforehand with prices that are too high, we can tell Serge, Ignacio, Wanda and Christine they don't have to come, and the rest of us will meet."

"I don't know. I have to think about it and I don't have time right now. I'm late to meet with Andrew and Jenny, and if I talk to you, you'll be taking my time away from your colleagues. You don't want that, do you?" with her dead frog-eye stare.

Meetings were a vehicle for asserting importance. "My time is like gold," she said, and told the assistants to schedule time far ahead for her and their managers to discuss agendas that would be determined later. Then she encouraged them to trade the time among themselves and was pleased to watch the market operate. She also was pleased to decline a meeting after it had been scheduled and rescheduled.

You, on the other hand, dared not cancel even if as the time neared you had nothing to discuss. She demanded an agenda a week in advance, not that she always bothered to look at it. This was hard, because topics often didn't come up until a couple days before the meeting. Design and construction move fast and you need to give answers now, not after a meeting in a week. But she had granted her time and would be damned if she'd cancel the chance to at least give you a lecture.

And athough she may have finally accepted a meeting, you could still be surprised. She called one day and said, "I want to know if I should come to today's meeting with PG&E."

"You don't have to; I can handle it. I've done this a couple of times before and—"

"Oh, I'm coming. I want to know if I should walk out the door and get in my car. Is the meeting going to take place?"

I was confused. Was she coming or not? Maybe she didn't know her mind until she talked about it. She told us we were confused because we didn't pay attention, and she told Leonora that she couldn't understand the simplest things. Poor Leonora grew quite flustered. I told her to let me speak for her as much as possible.

Deciphering the Boss

Now and then she would try to be, shall we say, proactive. Or maybe helpful. She left me a voicemail one morning.

"Margo Tuchman here, anticipating the one o'clock meeting about the parking lot and loop road at Hilltop College. I'd like to get on the second page about what we're going to talk about, how we're going to present it, particularly the graphics involved… [The signal cut out.] …visual…… ……Well I don't know if you know how… There are going to be people who have opinions, okay? So it'll be an opinion-laden discussion.

"Here are the graphics I'd like to be sure we have. Obviously the four layouts we got from GOCC that are hanging in the conference room, here in CPM, okay? Also I'd like the UE study that you and I looked at online, remember? I'd like us to plot that out in approximately the same size as the GOCC documents, okay. And finally here's something you're not familiar with. Actually two things.

"At Hilltop you're gonna need Karl's help with this or Mary's. You're gonna need the graphic of parking lot D which shows the dangerous intermingling of parking and circulation. We really need to be able to show… [The signal cut out.]

"If you have any questions call me on my cell phone or call Zora to get ahold of me because I'm going to be in back-to-back-to-back meetings, and you may or may not be able to actually reach me and so it will be just really important for you to reach me today or to get these things together, and I'd like to get a comfort zone, you know, some validation that you got this message and you are in fact working on getting these things and getting those things, and if you're not getting assistance from the people you need to get these things, then get me involved. But these things are relatively easy to get so I'm just hoping you don't have any issues, okay?"

Right, boss. Here's what you said: 1. You don't know if I know how to do something that vanished in the static. 2. This is a politically sensitive meeting. 3. Do this and do that.

4. Here's something else you don't know how to do. 5. Two things. 6. You need help. 7. You need these things. 8. I'm important; I'm in meetings all day. 9. Tell me you got this message. 10. Tell me you're doing what I told you to do since maybe you can't. 11. Tell me if you need me to boss somebody else around. 12. But this is all easy to do. I hope you can do it.

Here's another phone message verbatim. It's not worth trying to decipher.

"I'm looking at the October 14 GANTT chart that GOCC provided. [Two weeks earlier she had said she would look at it with her analyst-factotum Nora Beth.] I'm particularly looking for a very particular reason, at the site and landscape design-related activities, and as I'm looking at it, I see that they believe we've completed owner approval and direction related to landscape and site DDs, and they're now moving into the next phase, which is CDs; they've already moved into what they are gonna consider 50% CDs. You know, let me know if I'm crazy but in my mind I think we've seen early, maybe 50% SDs; and everything we've been doing since then has been value management. And in my mind, the next thing would be DDs. But you know, maybe in your mind or in GOCC's mind, there's no value in having DDs and we should go straight to CDs at this point. That's what it looks like we're gonna do if we believe this GANTT chart. And it also looks like we would have gotten landscape drawings on October 27, which was three days ago. And I think that if we had gotten anything, you would have told us the other day when we were with ya. So I'm just wondering where the heck we're at on this and the reason this is on my mind this particular moment is that I'm trying to figure out when I have a meeting with District-level people coming up. I have some routine meetings every month with them and I want to bring them some pictures of some of the crunchier things that've been in the last few years of particular interest to us, to include water features, the gateway entries, the amphitheater area, and in general, just sort of the overall kind of design, and I'm just wondering, so that's what I'm trying to do is do the work I have to do to report to the people that I need to report to. I'm trying to figure out how to make that happen I'm looking at this time frame on the GANTT chart. The GANTT chart makes no sense to me on a couple different levels in terms of time past we didn't get a deliverable and the deliverable wouldn't be what I'd be expecting anyway. So will you give me a call after you look at this and just let's talk about it, okay?"

I replied with a long email detailing who was doing what when, when deliverables were expected and review sessions were scheduled, GOCC's commitment to meet their proposed design and review schedule for the next three months if the District would give them timely answers and reviews, and their question about whether the District would insist on four separate reviews for the smaller projects.

She didn't respond. She probably didn't read beyond a couple paragraphs. But I'd answered the questions she'd asked, and I couldn't answer ones she hadn't, and I'd given her the amount of detail she always said she wanted.

A week later we were meeting with GOCC and their architect VQMR and she was ragging about us not keeping her up to date about the schedule. I finally said, "You didn't review GOCC's schedule that I gave you a month ago and then you left me a message suggesting that in my mind I was letting the contractor do less than the District standard. This project is moving forward, Margo, and the District needs to move with it unless they want to slow it down. What do you want to do at this point?"

She changed the subject.

After the meeting I told her I wasn't letting GOCC get away with anything and asked her to tell me if she thought I was not performing satisfactorily.

"You're doing okay," she said. "In my mind, it looked like GOCC wasn't going to give us the reviews that we want."

We seemed to part amicably, though who knows if it was amicable in her mind.

Staff Development

Susan from the facilities group asked Margo how to go about becoming a project manager. Margo said there was a chance if she could demonstrate a basic level of skill and told her to come back in three days with a reconciliation of expenditures from the first and second bond measures.

Susan worked evenings and most of the last night digging up figures from over sixty projects. She totaled budgets, appropriations and expenses, created a multi-colored spreadsheet, and brought it to Margo on the third morning.

Margo riffled through the papers and threw them on a table. "What is this? This is no good. A sophomore in college could do a better job than this. You're wasting my time. Come back when you have something worth looking at."

Susan left in tears.

Business Relationships

The District promoted business partnerships with local firms as a way to spend the bond funds in the community that had approved them. This also lessened contention with the labor unions. It also led to friendships.

The manager of the fire alarm company that did the District's work played guitar with Margo's husband. GOCC's regional vice president spent an occasional weekend with the Chancellor at the Tahoe house the Chancellor, Margo and Steve had bought as an investment.

The commissioning agent who did all the District's work invited Margo and Steve and their staff to an annual seminar that he held on a bus tour of wineries in Napa. A competent fellow, actually, who had done some work for BUEC while I was there. He told me he'd quit working for them. He hated giving up a client, but they were too nasty—the cutthroat partners took credit for his work, no one acknowledged his services, and the final straw was being blamed for a partner's oversight. I sympathized.

A certain consulting firm managed the procurement of furniture, fixtures, and equipment. My users complained that they didn't listen, were overbearing, left in the middle of meetings, didn't follow through or keep promises they made. The West Bay and Sepulveda PMs corroborated my experience and said their users were upset too. I passed the comments on to Margo and Steve and suggested that we try out someone else. At the next staff meeting Margo affirmed that we were going to continue using them as our sole consultant. It may have helped that the owner was a friend of hers.

There were some cozy relationships, but at least it wasn't full-scale corruption. Sometimes human nature sails close to the wind, but things get done, buildings get built, they don't fall down, and they function pretty well. There are boneheads and shirkers on a construction site but most everyone is pleased when the result looks good and runs smoothly. Besides which, what they do is visible—either it's neat and works or it doesn't. If a door doesn't swing or the latch gets jammed, everyone sees it. The designers—whose pride and reputation and future commissions depend on the final quality—are watching, and there are people on site whose only job is inspecting and testing. The subcontractor who installed the door fixes it. If they don't, they will not only not be hired for the next job, they may not be paid for this one. The worker who made the mistake will be fired if he messes up too often.

In a corrupt state of affairs quality doesn't matter because it's the favor that matters. I've been lucky not to have had to deal with that, but I've noticed that the amount of corruption is determined by the attitude of those at the top. When a president of the United States chooses to lie rather than tell the truth about even the most inconsequential things, soon the local sheriff will not own up to a mistake or even honest bafflement, citing reasons of security and fear of endangering his men. It's hard to keep corruption down when the bosses lie. Keep an eye on the top.

A PM Meeting

The project managers are meeting with Margo and Steve. Agenda item one, the District's design standards. Margo announces, "I busted my butt writing these guidelines and I expect you to bust your butts reading them, understanding them, and checking the design documents you get to make sure they comply with them." We nod.

Next item is collaboration with TND. Margo says, "Okay, as you know, some of us think that TND's shit stinks. Well, our shit stinks, too, so we're going to get along and learn how to work together." We nod.

Next: She and Steve ask us to report on whether our assistants are working up to snuff. We all give glowing reports. If we don't, she'll call them into private, airless meetings to berate them.

Next: Project manager issues. We raise none. She's not interested in our problems. Though she'll bitch at us later if one we didn't tell her about lands on her desk.

Worry

Don't worry. Be happy.

Good advice. You try it. Me, I worry.

I told Conrad that Margo didn't seem to trust my judgment. He said, "She needs a lot of communication or she gets nervous, and she has a good sense of the expectations and perceptions of various people in the District and wants to be sure they're being satisfied. If she didn't think you and Leonora were doing well you wouldn't be at Hilltop by yourselves, you'd be at West Bay where she could keep a closer watch on you. Same for the Sepulveda team. The West Bay staff isn't as experienced so she keeps them close. You shouldn't worry."

"Thanks," I said, "but whenever I've seen bosses talk to people the way she talks to me, they were fired soon after."

Margo was going to let another project manager's contract lapse in mid-January to save money, I heard; the company he worked for charged a lot for his services. Then again, he might have contradicted her too many times. Too bad; I liked him. We complained about her to each other and wondered what exactly our role was, since it didn't seem to be project management. We didn't manage the budget, for example—sometimes it was changed by someone and sometimes we were told later and sometimes we discovered it ourselves and had to ask who, when, and why. We couldn't act without her approval and couldn't get time to talk with her.

After him, me?

The VQMR architect asked me if she was dissatisfied with their performance—she seemed displeased all the time.

"Don't worry," I said, "it's her MO. She likes to intimidate people."

Maybe he stopped worrying.

Walkout

Margo, Steve, Leonora, the VQMR architect and I were meeting in CPM's windowless conference room. Margo was demanding to know why the architect had presented a certain paint color to the Hilltop cabinet, why I hadn't told him not to present it, why Leonora hadn't included color selection on the Outlook agenda, why Leonora was stuttering, why I'd let the Cabinet choose a color in the first place and that particular color in the second place, why I hadn't insisted that she attend the meeting she'd chosen to skip, whose start we had delayed ten minutes until she called to say she wasn't coming, why the architect hadn't insisted on meeting with her beforehand so she could have told him the color was unacceptable, when I was going to tell Cabinet that the rooms would be painted the color she would choose as soon as she got answers to these questions, why she had to vet everything her know-nothing staff touched, until the futility of further patient answers rose in my craw and I began gently and then more forcibly to say that we had been taking orderly steps with everyone's involvement but unfortunately sometimes what was important to some people was not communicated by them, and when that happened the proper thing to do was talk about the issue at hand, what could be done about it at this point, what the next steps would be, and hold the discussion in a calm and reasonable manner, everyone was doing their best and if she thought they weren't she should have a private discussion to tell them so and not attack them in front of others, my voice rising as I hit the table with my fist and said I had come to this place expecting to find a co-operative atmosphere where people supported each other as they worked toward a common goal and this kind of brutal-ity was unacceptable, and rising said that I would not stand for it and I was leaving for the day, and picked up my things and left the building and headed for my car.

Conrad was walking toward me and asked how things were going.

"I guess I just quit," I said.

"What happened?"

"I got tired of being beaten up by Margo and walked out of a meeting with her."

He looked distressed, and then looking beyond me said, "Here comes Steve."

Steve walked rapidly up and said, "I'm sorry, Jack. Are you leaving for good or will you come back to the meeting?"

"Well," I said, "I guess I don't feel like looking for another job. I'll come back."

Margo said nothing when we walked in, nor did she or Steve ever mention it.

A Good Boss

One afternoon I attended a meeting with the Hilltop cabinet, Ignacio, Margo and Steve. At one point I told the group, "Margo will probably chop my head off for this, but I'll tell you what I think we ought to do..."

Ignacio laughed and said, "Well, you just pick it up, put it back on, and keep going. We all make mistakes all the time."

I smiled and told them what I thought.

That evening as my wife and I were walking out to dinner, my phone rang. Ignacio said, "Jack, I don't want you to feel bad about this afternoon. Don't let that boss of yours get you down."

"Thank you. She is hard to deal with sometimes."

"If you ever need help, you just come to me."

That felt good.

He was a good guy. He began giving Susan small projects to manage that were funded with his own facilities money.

Tree Trimming

Margo wanted to have the trees at Hilltop trimmed. She told me to get a scope and price from an arborist she'd used before and tell GOCC to contract with him, not the landscape architect or subcontractor on their team, and to get the work done over the winter break when fewer people who might object to the desecration of trees would be on campus. GOCC didn't like it, since they'd have to help the arborist become signatory to the project labor agreement they were obligated to observe, run the new subcontract through their accounting and legal departments, provide safety training, oversee and schedule his work with no leverage since the deal was negotiated directly with the District, and so on. There wasn't much time, but we did arrange everything and got the work done.

In February Margo was walking around campus with me and saw the newly trimmed trees. "When did this happen?" she asked.

"We scrambled to get it done over the break."

"You should have waited until spring," she said. "That's when you should trim trees."

Campus Closure

On my first day of work, Leonora had handed me the contract with GOCC that Margo, Steve and Nora Beth had helped the chancellor and Ignacio finalize after several months of negotiation. Soon afterwards GOCC delivered the cost breakdown on which payments throughout the coming years would be based. After scrutiny by Nora Beth and me, the breakdown was approved.

A year into the job, Margo told me that the project included a means of closing the campus to vehicular traffic in an emergency. The gates across the two entrances were being removed as part of the landscaping work and needed to be replaced with something easy to use but less prominent than a gate. She had other things on her mind, she said, and other things needed to be done now, but I was not to forget it.

I looked through the contract documents. The only places I found campus closure mentioned were in the request for proposal and the first GOCC proposal. It appeared neither in the final contract's project description nor in the cost breakdown, so I figured that it had been deleted during negotiations to cut costs. I told this to Margo when I saw her next and got the frog stare and a change in subject.

Maybe not coincidentally, at that time she stepped up her demand that the CPM project teams produce the conformed documents she'd been asking for since forever. A conformed set incorporates the changes made during bidding—addenda, alternates that were accepted, changes in contract language—into the affected contract document so that it can be read without needing to refer to the several documents recording each change.

I told GOCC's project manager that Margo had me and Leonora working on it. "Why?" she asked. "Everything is documented and we're a year into the job."

"Go figure. But we have to give it a crack."

"But then I'll have to review it. It's a waste of time. Talk her out of it."

I tried, because I too thought it a waste of time. You wanna build the best project you can by addressing design and construction issues as they come up, or you wanna have the best documents you can saying how to do what had already been done? But Margo was adamant, so we produced a set. When she finally sat down weeks later to look at it, she wasn't satisfied. She told Leonora to change several things by herself so I could work on other things. But poor Leonora didn't know much about design and construction and needed help with everything. Margo found fault with this version too.

This went on for several months, Margo complaining that none of the other PMs had completed theirs, either. I kept a discussion of our latest version on our meeting agendas until she finally said she'd given up, none of us seemed to care; though she did admit that Leonora and I had gotten farther than anyone else.

In the meantime, my projects were well beyond the halfway point and it was clear that the contingencies had plenty of unneeded money. District leadership took advantage of this to landscape areas that had been removed during the negotiations, repave roads and parking lots, and do other work the Hilltop cabinet thought was important.

Margo kept reminding me about the campus closure and finally asked for a meeting to discuss it with GOCC. She told us what she had in mind and asked us to work on a design. I was to meet with campus security and facilities to get their input. GOCC assumed, as did I, that there would be a change order for it as for other added work. Margo said nothing one way or the other but talked as if it was part of the base contract and told GOCC not to have their landscape architect design it. "Jack will do it himself. It's easy."

I decided I'd better clarify the contractual situation. I double-checked the documents and called Mary Beth. She checked them too and confirmed that it must have been dropped during the negotiations. I told Margo during one of my meetings with her that whether it had been or not, the fact was that it wasn't in the contract now. I got the frog stare again and she said, "If you guys had produced the conformed set, we wouldn't have this problem."

"The conformed set is ready, and we're ready to review it with you. Shall we look at it now?"

"Did you meet with campus security and facilities?"

"Yes, and we developed your ideas. Security asked for such and such and facilities for thus and so."

"I need to be involved in this and I don't have time now. Put it on the next agenda."

And so it went.

I selected bollards, figured out how to install a removable one in the middle of the street and where to store it when not in use, chose a paint color, a chain, a box to store it in, met with security and facilities again, changed things, met with Margo, changed the color, joined her at West Bay to review their mockup, where she directed the contractor to move the bollards they'd installed, heard from West Bay security that a chain of plastic rather than metal would be easier to move around, talked to Hilltop security and changed the material to plastic, chose a color, asked for her approval, was told that she was assigning oversight to Steve since she was so busy. That complicated things because she still had to review whatever he approved.

At Steve's request I walked the sites with the contractor to take photos and prepared a plan showing bollard and underground storage box locations, showed it to Steve, walked the sites with him, revised the plan and photos, showed Margo, revised the plan and photos, tried to find plastic reflective ribbons or triangles to attach to the chain to make it more visible at night.

Time passed, the rest of the work was complete, the subcontractors left, only four or five GOCC people remained, Ignacio wanted to close out the project, and Margo wouldn't approve the as-built documents GOCC had submitted several times, so GOCC asked for a meeting with Ignacio to talk about how to finish up.

There was some paperwork to complete, lien releases and the last as-built documents to submit, a couple construction items to finish, and a couple District requests for additional work including the campus closure system. Ignacio said to forget about campus closure.

Useless Work

Our materials testing lab's fee needed a small augmentation. Steve asked Leonora to prepare an entirely new contract with additional safeguards against poor performance, though they had done a fine job and little remained to do. It made no difference and it took her away from things that did.

The users were moving into their new building and someone was calling every twenty minutes to ask for one thing or another. Margo chose this moment to make Leonora spend a week at West Bay listing the drawings that were to have been submitted at early phases of the project—an utter waste of time, since drawings in later phases superseded the earlier ones. But if in Margo's judgment the lists had to be made, couldn't she have waited a few days? Wasn't our fundamental role getting people into a new space? Nope. We had to keep things orderly. It was like rearranging deck chairs on a ship that had sunk, while the one full of passengers sailed on by.

Overall, I think Steve and Margo wasted a third of our time, though in the end I suppose it didn't matter. Everything got built, on time and on budget, the users were happy, the cabinet was happy, the District and contractors and subs were happy. But it would all have been more relaxed if we could have concentrated on things that did matter.

Some Advice

Aesop say: The mouse who out of compassion gnawed the net that held the lion was unexpectedly aided by the lion.

Aesop say: The horse who out of compassion carried the snake across the river was bitten by the snake, who excused himself by saying that it was his nature.

Human nature includes the mouse and the snake. Which do you prefer?

Benjamin Franklin say: Treat all young women with respect because you don't know who they're going to marry. (He also said he courted older women because they were more appreciative. By older he meant thirties. (How old, by the way, is a woman of a certain age? Those days, probably thirties. These days, forties or fifties?))

I say: Young women, old women, bad bosses, total strangers—let's be civil to each other. We lie in the bed we make, right? You wanna deal with uncivil people all day long? You think they wanna deal with your surliness? As ye sow so shall ye reap.

Need some reasons for treating strangers with respect? 1. You don't descend to their sniveling level. 2. You don't know what they might do for you if so disposed or to you if indisposed. 3. You don't know who they may become. 4. You don't know who may hear of how you treated them. 5. You promote rationality and reason. 6. You develop a good reputation.

At the main building's dedication ceremony a woman of a certain age detached herself from two other ladies and pulled me aside. "I want to pass on a compliment, because they are so rare these days: People tell me you are a gentleman. I've heard how politely you acted with a very difficult person. Everyone who saw it was impressed."

That was lovely.

Margo's Final Jab

As construction was completed, staff were informed that they should look for other jobs. Steve told me that I would be let go mid-June and in the meantime I should work just three days a week so that what remained of my fee would last until then. I must say, I took a quick liking to four days off each week.

I called people I knew, including TND's vice president, who had been at Berkeley while I was at UCOP. Hilltop's president liked what I'd done and called Ignacio. He called TND's VP. TND's construction manager at Hilltop also called. The upshot was that TND offered me a job as planner for the District's third bond program. My income would be half what it had been and could be as an independent contractor, but they agreed to a three-day workweek and I thought that even if their NCCD contract evaporated I had a better chance with them than finding something on my own. They had more contacts, a marketing department, other projects I could work on, and if worse came to worst I could, having been employed, collect unemployment insurance. They arranged for me to start the first of July and Ignacio directed Margo and Steve to keep me until then.

The last week of June I walked into a CPM staff meeting at West Bay. Someone asked how I was.

"Fine," I said. "I have a job."

Margo said darkly, "But not for long."

I didn't understand what she meant. My job with CPM was ending in a week? She didn't know I was going to TND? I wouldn't last long with them? Their contract with NCCD was in jeopardy? She thought passage of the third bond measure on November's ballot was unlikely? But what she meant no longer mattered, and I wasn't curious enough to ask.

In the end I had the last laugh. In August Ignacio told her that her last day would be September thirtieth. I had outlasted her.

And Yet

When Ignacio praised her for everything she'd accomplished at an impromptu going-away lunch he organized, she cried. I was touched. She was a human being after all, she had cared, she'd tried as best she could.

But then, Attila also accomplished things. But Attila wasn't in the public sector—private bosses can do what they want as long as they're making a profit. How do public bosses get around oversight and accountability for abuse?

Ignoring for the moment that public institutions depend ultimately on funding controlled by the wealthy and hence share an ethos where mistreatment of employees is not necessarily frowned upon, bosses succeed when they keep the system running. Their flaws are forgiven when they talk the right talk, cover their bosses' asses, show dedication to the institution's values. Promotions are based on how much influential people like you, and they like you when you resemble them. You can rise higher in the public sector based on good work alone, but to get to the upper levels you have to show commitment to the values of the greater system of wealth. At those levels, commitment is just as unthinking and unquestioning as in the private.

Private Sector V :
Back on the Street Again

Ignacio had already met with the three college cabinets to see what projects they wanted. Two TND colleagures and I fleshed out the projects, estimated costs, chose locations, and decided when to build them. Another guy and I rewrote Margo's design standards to align more with industry standards, and we started in on rewriting the design-build contracts and the design professional selection procedure.

The bond measure in November failed and TND laid me off the following morning.

Time for unemployment compensation. Nope–turned out you had to have been working for somebody during the two previous quarters and I'd been self-employed. If you want to benefit from the system, you can't leave it for a minute.

Hiring Policies

You probably know this already, but I had to ask around: How do bad bosses get their jobs?

May dad said, "The wealthy will do anything they must to keep their wealth, so they hire people who won't rock the boat. This matters more than doing a good job or treating others fairly."

The Rich
say what they want

Directors
issue commands

Managers
figure out how to do it and make sure it gets done by command, coercion, exhortation, suggestion, consensus-building, whatever works

Workers
do it

My brother-in-law said, "Ninety-nine percent of people are assholes, so chances are good your boss will be one."

"That's well and good," I said, "but how does it play out in the workplace? You teach in a school, where presumably cooperation and decency are prized—how do the assholes get promoted?"

"Good people turn down managerial positions out of distaste," my sister said, "just like they won't run for office, so what's left are the bad ones. Aggressive people push themselves forward, some people charm and flatter, and some keep a low inoffensive profile and outlast everyone else. They all do their work well enough to show they're not incompetent, though they don't have to be accomplished themselves—workers are for that. Sometimes mistakes are made—a good person is promoted into a role she can't fill and there she stays unhappy and a trial to her subordinates until she retires, or, if her incompetence is too destructive, until she's transferred someplace where she can do less damage."

"People are hired and promoted from within the group because what matters most is to be known," my brother-in-law said. "If newcomers don't fit in, it's not a fun place to be. But people have their own reasons for staying and do whatever it takes, usually shutting up and lying low."

Job Satisfaction

Changing jobs every three years or so brings not only raises and higher positions but broader experience, which is good for yourself and makes you more attractive to employers—up to a point: If you move too often or past the age of thirty-five, they begin to wonder if you're a job-hopper, if there's something wrong with you. Can't you get along with people? Are you incompetent or lazy? The story you tell about why you're moving has to end with wanting to settle down now and dedicate yourself to serving what you think is the best company in the field.

Another benefit is that you don't have to suffer the same fool for too long. There is some satisfaction in leaving one for another, and during the time it takes to plumb the foolishness of the next you can enjoy the sparkle of new systems and people.

Then too, when your nose is dulled by the odor of the butt in front of you, it's wonderful to soar above the circling jackasses as you travel from one work gang to another in the free mode of life between two jobs like Sisyphus atop his hill watching the rock roll down, that soaring moment another pearl on the string of life that will have been worth living when you tell your final rosary. But still, it ain't fair that the asses have a monthly string of pension checks while I must join yet another dusty circle.

What to Look for in a Job

Sit outside on a warm night and ponder the rising moon which shone upon all men who lived before and all their ancient ancestors unto the archaic plankton and elemental rock and will shine upon our unimaginable descendents and still later upon the rock which will outlast us all, and gaze at the unfathomable stars in blackness deep beyond the bounds of what our minds can grasp. The workplace is very small. And yet it matters.

Find something you like doing and find the place that lets you do it most. Be aware that you serve the aims of the organization your work for. Find one whose central aim most closely aligns with your values and work for it. You'll work hard anywhere so work where you're happiest. Remember that nothing's perfect.

Your average workers, no matter whether public or private sector, resemble their counterparts in the other. They are all just trying to do a good job and get along. Private workers are edgier, maybe, quicker to innovate, keener, because those qualities are rewarded. Public ones are more relaxed, but despite corporate propaganda to the contrary, they're not lazier. You find incompetence everywhere. There's the same amount of backstabbing but more hypocrisy on the public side, since avarice is less acceptable than on the private. On the public, other values like service and education still have some importance. You tend to have more latitude for thought and action in a governmental or educational system.

Size makes a difference. Bureaucracies generally have more restraints on bad behavior than small companies. A small agency, given that it's part of a government, may be the topological equivalent of a large company in having niches for more types of people.

The external threat to private companies is competition from other companies expanding into their territory; to public organizations it is loss of funding. Politics for private companies means influencing public policy for the companies' gain. Politics for public organizations means influencing policy for the maintenance or increase of funding.

The private side's basic motivator is profit; the public side's is service. Private employees are more driven by personal greed—for salary, bonus, perquisites—; public employees more by desire for power and authority. On the private side you can become wealthy. On the public side, influential.

Marketing and sales are important in the private sector. You have proposals, presentations, lunches and parties. Call, email, get on the team. In the public sector, people are selling to you. You can be cool, low-key, sincere, patronizing, condescending.

PRIVATE SECTOR VI :
DECENCY VS AMBITION

Two people called with job leads, but one was too far away and I disliked the other boss, and I only wanted to work three days a week doing something I liked. Getting mighty picky and choosy, I was.

Expert witnesses are highly paid for intermittent work and my hair was gray enough to pass for one, so I called Norman Manchester, who'd done that sort of thing. Though I hadn't been fond of Norman, I will say this for him: He'd had the integrity or spirit or ambition to leave BUEC and open a branch office for a Portland engineering company named QBF, bringing along two good people, Max the marketing guy and Nicco the great young engineer. Norman gave me the name of someone to call, and we kept talking, and the upshot was that QBF Consulting Engineers hired me on contract three days a week to do commissioning and anything else that came up.

After two months the Portland principals told Norman I was too expensive and they wanted me to become permanent staff. The wage would be a third lower than my billing rate but part-time was okay and I'd have benefits. I felt as I had with TND that the position would be steady and if I turned it down I'd soon be looking for another, and I do hate looking for work, and whatever I found would probably be full time. I told him and Nicco they should know I wasn't much of a salesman and my design skills were out of date. That was all right—they wanted someone who was good with clients and could manage projects. Norman said he would support a quick promotion to senior associate if I worked full time;

I said thanks but no, I wanted time for publishing. Thus I signed up.

It was a good company and truly was at the forefront of sustainable building design, unlike Haravan which only claimed to be. "Remember when Haravan rebranded itself?" Max recalled. "Tom Thompson told me he knew that they weren't particularly skilled in green design, but if their marketing said they were, people would believe it. And they did. I started getting phone calls from people who said they'd never known." Simple as that.

QBF's president told us that most of our clients were repeats. "Do a good job," he said, "and have some fun while you're at it. There will always be work. We're not trying to be the biggest firm in the Northwest, only the best." It was nice to hear that from the top.

But Norman's enthusiasms lay elsewhere. His talents were schmoozing, scheming and selling, and his only goal was to grow the office. His management style hadn't changed—while he wheeled and dealed, Nicco ran the place, designed, oversaw production, wrote proposals, dealt with clients, ran the staff meetings, did the work. I was glad it wasn't me this time.

Norman shared a curious trait with the Haravan partners: They would speak frankly about people only up to a certain point. Now, project managers are very open, even gossipy, about their clients, consultants, contractors, bosses. A PM's success depends on how well he gets people to work toward completing his project, and the more he knows about them— who does a good job, who is unreliable, who argues about what in what manner—the better he can choose the right ones and the better direct the circus.

Engineers, on the other hand, are uneasy talking about people. Maybe they think personality is irrelevant—after all, their success depends largely on fitting together the jigsaw puzzle of a system whose pieces are called into being through pure thought. They hate to be inaccurate—it erodes their self-esteem and appearance of infallibility—; maybe they hesitate before the imprecision of character judgment. Or they're afraid to be overheard saying anything denigratory because their livelihood depends on the good opinion of everyone who is or might be or might influence a client. But there has to be honest character assessment to run an enterprise, doesn't there? Maybe not—maybe it doesn't matter in small engineering firms. Or maybe it does and that's why they're small.

Or maybe salesmen classify people not by how they perform but by how they can be influenced. The mark's character matters only insofar as it affects the imposition of the salesman's will. At any rate, I learned to keep certain opinions to myself.

No one wore ties at QBF, even to interviews, because none of the clients wore ties. In fact, the Silicon Valley social media companies wore shorts, T-shirts and sandals. Heck, those companies launder your clothes, repair your bicycle, cut your hair and feed you for free. They're Mommy! You're there to work and they're there to ease your way. And no booze anywhere. Are you kidding? The low-cost cafeterias and clothing shops of the defense contractors have some catching up to do.

I published and edited and wrote at home Friday through Monday and went to the office on Tuesday. It was a new experience to not be at the center of things. I was used to working on the most prominent projects, but now I did small or unusual jobs like training a client's maintenance staff in their geothermal system's operation, and I spent a fair amount of time writing proposals for new commissioning work. I studied building plans and devised equipment tests.

Commissioning work is strung out over many months and sometimes there wasn't much to do. We offered my services to Portland for quality assurance reviews but they didn't take us up on it. Norman asked me to develop a marketing presentation on commissioning and to investigate operating problems on a project of his. Shades of BUEC. However, he said the Portland guys wanted part-time employees to be fully billable so I shouldn't charge to administration or marketing or to the problem project, whose fees were expended; but he was vague when I asked where I should.

New employees were flown to Portland for introductions but after a year I still hadn't visited. Norman stopped taking me on marketing presentations and seemed disappointed with my failure to solve the operating problems. Owen, a Portland principal, came down, and he and Norman fired a young engineer who'd been there since I started. Nicco told me they were disappointed that she hadn't been as experienced as she'd made herself out to be when they hired her. I began to worry. I looked at myself and saw an oldish stranger who had wandered in from the street, a nice, helpful, semi-retired fellow who wasn't on a career path and wasn't really part of the office. The commissioning guy in Portland was semi-retired too, but he'd been a principal; I had the drawback of not being semi-retired from QBF. I wanted to stay until I did retire and hoped they wouldn't find me dispensable before they got used to having me around.

I took Nicco out for coffee to see if anything was in the air. "I don't feel like I'm completely part of the office," I told him, "which of course is to be expected since I'm not here all the time and can't work on the larger projects, but I'm sorry more of my skills aren't being used."

"What do you want to do?"

"Commissioning, but I'm running out of work. I could help with fire protection but I'm out of date. Peer reviews, I'm good at that, but Portland isn't giving me any work. Sometimes they don't even return my calls."

"Well, sometimes they don't return mine; they're pretty busy. I know they'd like your help. Why don't you call Nate and ask if you can help with the commissioning standards?"

"I can also help with marketing, but Norman said I shouldn't charge time to it, and he said not to bill my Cardiff time. I don't know what to do. It seems to me it's better to bill our time accurately so we know what we spent it on."

"I think so too," he said. "I'll talk to Norman. He and I will deal with Portland about your nonbillable time."

A couple days later he and Norman told me that Portland wanted me to attend a seminar in the fall on fire sprinkler design to bring my skills up to date. The two of them wanted me to join them when delivering the net-zero buildings marketing presentation, and they had reminded Portland that I was available for peer reviews.

That was reassuring, but I grew uneasy again when Norman hired Kevin Quincy. KQ was a go-getter in his early thirties, long hair swept back, four-day growth of beard, stylish glasses and shoes, all about sales and who he knew and what he'd done. He'd run an office in China.

"Where was it?" I asked. I'd done a project there once.

"What I did was spend two weeks in Oakland and then two weeks travelling between three cities in China."

That was an office?

His parents were professors. I asked what they taught. His father taught urban planning. Where? He hesitated and then told me. I looked it up—it was a Christian college and I couldn't find anyone on the faculty with his name, and the single urban planning course was buried in the social studies department and taught how to proselytize in cities. I later found out that he had graduated from there himself.

He got along with Norman like a house on fire. They told stories about sales they'd made and strategized about marketing and how to grow the office, who to hire, and how to entice them. KQ giggled at everything Norman said. In three weeks he became our human resources manager and took over running the staff meetings. They fired a guy who'd started five months earlier. KQ explained that he hadn't fit into the company culture and would be happier in a larger organization, which may have been true, but Nicco told me that Norman was disappointed that he hadn't brought in the work they'd expected. I'd brought in nothing but a few additional services.

Norman got a job to inspect a building's infrastructure. KQ took an electrical engineer and a junior mechanical to walk the building, and then he and Norman brainstormed recommendations that would lead to further work for us.

They called me in and asked me to estimate the remaining useful equipment lifetime using industry standards and KQ's notes and photos.

Easy enough. But KQ's notes were barely intelligible and there were only five photos of two pieces of equipment. I asked if he had more.

"Ask Evan to put his on the server," he said.

Evan had eighty photos of distribution panels, nameplates and switches. I told KQ, "Evan only took pictures of electrical stuff. We don't have any of mechanical."

"Oh. I saw that somebody was taking pictures so I didn't bother."

"Okay. Then I'll compare the installation dates you wrote down to the ASHRAE lifetimes."

Two hours later I handed him a list of the equipment with expected remaining years of operation. "Where are your recommendations?" he asked.

"What recommendations?"

"Whether they should replace the equipment."

"KQ, I didn't know you wanted recommendations, and I'm not sure how to make any. I didn't see the equipment and I don't know what shape it's in. All I have to go on is ASHRAE's lifetimes."

"I want a paragraph on each piece of equipment discussing its condition and recommending replacement or not."

"Well, I can't make things up, but I can format a report and if you'll sit down with me to tell me what you saw, I can take it from there." He assented.

Mid-afternoon I told him I was done, but he didn't have time. When I left for the day I asked if he'd looked at it.

"I'll look at it tonight," he said.

"Email me, and I'll work on it over the weekend." He assented.

The weekend passed with no response.

Tuesday morning he asked if I was done. "No," I said, "I was waiting for your comments."

"What? It's due tomorrow."

"Well, I checked twice a day hoping to hear from you. I need your help unless you want me to fake it. I can do that, if you want."

"No, I don't want you to fake it," he said. "I can't talk now, I have to get on a call. Are you going to be here when I'm done?"

"When are you done?"

He walked briskly away. Five minutes later he sent an email: "My bad. I didn't communicate like I should. Can we meet at 11?"

So we met, he read what I'd written and gave me information, and I wrote the report.

He mostly ignored me after that. He whispered to Norman or Nicco, who both sat across from me. He joked around with Terry who was buying a house and having a baby, Iannos who was getting married, Max who golfed with potential clients. KQ had just gotten remarried and was having another baby, knew all about buying houses, had golfed for years. He started an EMBA program, executive MBA for those of us who didn't know, and promised to share the exciting new ideas he would be learning. Copies of *Harvard Business Review* and *Bloomberg Businessweek* were neatly arranged on his desk. I decided to see what I could learn instead of detesting him.

He asked me to write a commissioning proposal to a client of his. I had to ask a week later if he'd sent it.

"Oh, I sent it last week."

"Did you change anything?"

He muttered something about a couple little things. "Can I see it? I'd like to keep track."

"It's on the network." But the only thing on the network was my version.

Ivan quit, telling me that Norman didn't like him, and he didn't like the turn the office was taking. Tattooed Bob decided to move to Nevada and Norman and KQ were not unhappy. The office size was back to the eight it had been when I started but there was one less engineer and one more salesman.

Nicco and KQ did my performance review. Performance: Excellent, helps the younger engineers—they look up to you; walk around and see how you can help. My short term goals: More commissioning, need work, when you're out marketing be sure to mention it. Peer reviews, I'm good at them. Do you like doing them? It does get boring if there's too much. Fire protection, the seminar will brush me up and I can help Portland and sign drawings in California without fear of getting us into trouble. Project management, I'm good at that but since I'm not in the office all five days we have to find the right job. Long term goals: Here Nicco told KQ, "Jack's experience is unusual. He's been a mechanical engineer, fire protection engineer, a principal—he was my boss at Haravan and BUEC—he's been on the owner's side, he knows higher ed... Tell us what you want to do now, Jack."

Assuming he'd asked for KQ's sake and taking the opportunity to reassure KQ that I wasn't a competitor, I gave an answer that someone had once given me. "Well, you know, I'm not trying to build a career. I've had one. What I want to do now is put my knowledge and experience at the service of a good group of people I like working with."

KQ didn't react. To break the silence I said, "I owe you an apology for the way I acted about that report."

"What happened?" Nicco glanced at us.

I summarized. "So Tuesday morning KQ and I puffed our chests out at each other, and I've felt bad ever since. That wasn't right of me."

KQ looked like he didn't know what to say. I said, "I have to say I admire how you get your team together at the beginning of a project to tell them their roles, the client's goals, the milestones, so they know what to expect." Our CAD guy had told me after one of those briefings that he thought KQ talked too much, but the point now was to reinforce good habits, not suggest improvements. Plus a bit of flattery. "You're a good communicator," I said. "People appreciate it."

He looked pleased. Nicco told me they were giving me a four percent raise.

"Thanks. And by the way," I told KQ, "Norman told me to bill my Cardiff time to 636 Nancy."

"Cutting into my profit, is he?" Two weeks later he insisted on seeing a proposal I was writing and billed a day's time to its marketing number.

They finally arranged a trip to Portland. I had several good conversations, they asked me to review a couple projects, and the president apologized when he realized that I hadn't been there before.

I was on good terms with people in the building business: project managers public and private, directors of design and construction, architects in different fields, operations and maintenance chiefs. I stayed in touch with the ones I liked and the ones I didn't dislike who might be useful one day, telling them what I was up to, maintaining friendly relations without offering services, leaving business out of it until there might be a strong reason to ask a favor. Now of course old business acquaintances do no good unless called upon, and of course I want to work with clients I like, but I didn't trust Norman and KQ. If I was let go after I brought in a job with a friend who expected to work with me, I'd have done him a disservice and lost his trust.

I set up a presentation at a UC campus and Norman and KQ invited me to strategize for it. Higher ed people in general are put off by flashy salesmen and appreciate a relaxed discussion of the topic at hand, and UC people in particular respond to former insiders. Relationships are best nurtured in a certain style. In fact, Haravan had gotten no work in higher ed after I left because they never learned how to act. I talked Norman and KQ out of as many suggestions as I could, and was only mildly embarrassed by them at the campus.

They didn't care about my contacts at VQMR since KQ

already knew the people who mattered, but they pushed for introductions to anyone else. Someone gave Norman the name of the data center construction director at a large company. I overheard Norman telling KQ about it and that he'd sent some marketing material, so I said, "Oh, I know that guy. Why don't I have lunch with him?"

He was a friend I hadn't seen for a while, and he told me to tell Norman that the two of us could take care of things. It was fun to catch up and interesting to hear about the changes he was making at the company which included, he hoped, working with some new designers.

Norman pressed me for a lunch to introduce him and our Portland data center designer to my friend and his design director. He was very hush hush about it all. I arranged it, and then I overheard him telling KQ about the meeting he'd set up. When my friend had to postpone, I overheard him quietly telling the Portland fellow that the meeting needed to be rescheduled. He didn't seem to want anyone to know that I was involved.

I mentioned to Max the marketing guy that it felt like Norman was pretending to be our contact with the company. Max told me that the guy who'd given Norman my friend's name had actually given it to him and he'd given it to Norman, and Norman was also pretending to be an old friend of Max's friend. "And KQ just asked me to start sharing my leads, since he needs to know everything that's going on. Iannos told me KQ told him not to bother calling his contacts because he'd do it from now on. I introduced him to Norman and encouraged Norman to hire him, and now he's acting like an asshole. What, is he taking over the office?"

"My wife thinks he's insecure about his position."

"Maybe, but he's still an asshole. I think I'm going to have to look for a job. Owen asked Norman what I spend my time doing, and Norman said he didn't know. Owen's coming to San Francisco to talk with us."

Owen was one of the Portland partners. I called him to ask for fifteen minutes when he came.

I began by telling Owen how good Nicco was: He ran the office, made sure the designers knew what to do, oversaw office supplies, marketed and wrote proposals, and designed projects on top of everything else. He needed all the support they could give him. Owen nodded and made a note.

"Norman's not interested in the office," I went on. "He's only interested in selling jobs, and KQ is the same. Of course we need people who can bring in work, but Nicco's the only one watching the office."

"Norman is sort of beyond that, isn't he. He's done it all and now he wants to do what he does best."

"Sure, and selling is one of a principal's main tasks. And KQ is energetic, but he's not much of a leader."

"KQ needs experience, but we need energy to grow the office."

"Something that bothers me is that when I call old friends and arrange meetings, KQ and Norman take the credit for it. In the end it doesn't matter who brings in work, but it doesn't feel good to have them take over. Max too, well, Max can speak for himself, but he was the one Holloway called with the winery job, and Norman took credit for that."

"That comes up in Portland sometimes. People get protective of client relationships they've built up and are offended when someone else starts working with them."

"Sure, it happens. Well, support Nicco and Max. They're the reason I came here."

Owen looked at me. "Max doesn't have other skills like you do."

That didn't bode well, but I let it drop though I'd have liked to say more. I could have asked how many projects KQ had brought in (none), or told him how relaxed and cheerful everyone was when Norman and KQ were away and how silence descended when either arrived. Or about our CAD guy telling me he was upset at KQ for not giving him directions on the winery project and thinking it might be time to look around. Or the designer who asked for help and was asked in response, "What do you think?" since KQ didn't know and was fishing for a clue.

I could have told Owen how Norman and KQ mocked Portland's stuffy attitudes and schemed to hide their intentions to get what they wanted, or their disdain for the company's philosophy statement committing them to dignity, respect and valuing the contributions of others.

But you can't say too much at once, and you have to let people figure some things out on their own. It was at least good to know that the Portland principals were aware of some failings.

Max heard of a job at the UC campus where we had presented for which the mechanical engineer would assemble the design team. He and I told Norman that responding to the RFQ would reinforce the campus's awareness of us and that we could ask VQMR to join us, which would at the very least show VQMR we were serious about wanting to work with them. Norman agreed, so Max and I started getting in touch with the other consultants.

KQ arrived later and demanded to know why we were spending our time on it. "Who approved this?" "I did," Norman said. KQ backed off but asked how much effort we were planning to spend on it, what we would get out of it, if the marketing group had the resources to work on it, what chance we had of getting it. After a while I lost my patience. "Look, I don't give a damn. You decide. If you don't want us to go after it, just say so."

He reared back and said, "Jack, you and I need to talk. Come with me." He headed for the conference room.

"Let's ask Nicco to join us."

"No. You and I need to talk."

He'd learned the bully tricks fast, but what the hell—I was a big boy.

He glared at me. "It's clear that you and I don't agree on a lot of things, but that's not something that should be public."

It was all very familiar. I decided not to help him, to say nothing until he said something sensible.

Finally he said, "I've figured out how to deal with everyone else here, but I don't know what makes you tick."

It's all about you, isn't it, I didn't say.

"I'm here to help you," he said. "What can I do to support you?"

"You don't need to support me. I'm here to support you. How can I do that?"

"Look," he said, "I feel like you're not part of the office. Would you consider working five days a week?"

To make you feel more comfortable with me? My foot. And by the way, if I work five days, I'll work as a project manager where I can have fun and make good money. "KQ, I'm here because I want to work with a good group of people and I'm working three days so I can do some other things I've waited all my life to do."

He was very nonplussed. "Well, you and I have to reach some kind of understanding. What can I do to improve things?"

He said the things a sincere person would say, but he was fishing for the things that made me tick so he could couch his talk to me in my own terms so I would think he shared my outlook. I was briefly tempted to tell him a few truths; but if he saw any of the truth in them he would be insulted.

"Listen to people," I said. "They have things to offer. They want to be heard. You don't have to agree, but you ought to listen."

"I will listen, but I'll tell you now that I may not agree."

"People have different ideas. It's good to share them."

"Yes, but you have to know that in the end an office is not a democracy."

He must have learned that in an EMBA class.

Three weeks later they fired Max.

I asked Iannos if Max was on vacation, since I hadn't seen him all week. "KQ told me he's transitioning to a part-time job."

"Oh no, I'm sorry."

"Me too."

KQ took me aside a few minutes later to tell me that though it wasn't common knowledge yet, he wanted to let me know that despite Max's valuable contacts, he hadn't brought in anything for months in this hot job market, and he was the chief marketing officer!

"Thank you for telling me," I said. He had certainly gained my esteem by sharing that confidence.

I called Max. Max was angry. "They gave me a contract for ten hours a week for four weeks. After the meeting with Owen, Norman told me he was surprised; he hadn't known this was coming. That's bullshit. If he hadn't known, he would have been pissed off that they decided without consulting him. He's the managing principal! He was pretending that he had nothing to do with it."

"Are you kidding? He was the one who decided to do it. Him and KQ."

"KQ! Let me tell you, don't trust KQ."

"He told me they let you go because you hadn't brought in any work for six months."

"What? They didn't even ask me what work I'd brought in!" He named three projects. "And KQ took credit for them. You know what Norman does? He hears of a job and puts it on the list with a high fee and probability so his projected backlog looks good. And KQ puts my leads on his list so it looks like he found them. I tell you, don't trust him. Why should I work to promote his career? I asked Nicco if KQ is taking over. He said KQ is trying to get him to take over the winery job now that it's in design and he's out of the office so much. He hasn't even been to a staffing meeting in weeks, and Nicco is running them again. I thought KQ was supposed to take some of the load off Nicco's shoulders."

"Yeah, this is really chickenshit. I just read an article saying small engineering firms are deciding to do without dedicated marketing people. Maybe they're just following the trend."

"I could understand a business decision. I wouldn't mind that. But they're hiring this new kid, this marketing assistant, and they have two in Portland, and that's all Norman and KQ do. It wasn't a business decision."

"I know. Maybe it's time for me to look around too."

"Are you thinking of leaving?"

"If Nicco leaves, I will."

"I can talk to so-and-so [who ran another engineering firm]."

"If I leave, I'll look for a PM job. It's more fun than this."

"I'm having lunch with so-and-so [who ran a project management company] on Thursday. He's busy and he's always looking for good people. Or I can talk to so-and-so, who's opening a branch for Such-and-Such Architects. He's trying to staff the office."

"Thanks, Max. I think I'll wait until after the holidays and see what my bonus is. I owe these guys a sprinkler design after the seminar they're sending me to, anyway. But then I'll see."

The marketing assistant started the next week and Norman and KQ loaded him up with some of the tasks Max used to do. KQ grew expansive. Max was gone, he'd reached a truce with me, he was taking the upper hand with Nicco, he'd get a large bonus for his great work, Norman would retire in two years, he would run the office for a while and then move on to a larger pond, a shining example of business success.

So here I am. Decent job out of the ditches, one of a fairly small group who know how to do it, not all that well paid but enough, good people and values in the main office, good people in this promising branch except for two asses slowly wrecking its camaraderie and dedication to good work and chances of standing out from the competition.

Maybe it's time to soar again. Things always change and I'll do just fine when they do. If worse comes to worst I can be a paperboy again, and with luck I can do it from a bicycle.

Moral

To survive at work, silence alone is insufficient. Cunning offends my sense of honesty. Exile is uncomfortable. The internal consistency of art is wonderful. Work is not art.

Long live art!

www.ingramcontent.com/pod-product-compliance
Lightning Source LLC
LaVergne TN
LVHW091303080426
835510LV00007B/372